Study Guide for Decoding 1984

With Typical Questions and Answers

Steven Smith

Sherwood Press

CONTENTS

How To Use This Guide

This analysis of "1984" by George Orwell intends to offer a study guide to readers who need a more in-depth view of the story.

This book is divided into questions, so the answers appear in a short essay style and may include repeated information. The questions are typical of what a high school student may experience.

I want to think all important questions have been either directly or indirectly answered. However, if you, the reader, feel something is missing, please reach out to me, and I will add it!

Happy studying!

Steven Smith

stevensmithvo@gmail.com

www.classicbooksexplained.com

HISTORICAL BACKGROUND TO THE NOVEL "1984"

George Orwell's "1984" is a dystopian novel set in a totalitarian state. Written in 1948 and published in 1949, its themes and ideas emerge from a variety of historical, political, and personal contexts. Understanding this historical tapestry is essential for appreciating the depth of Orwell's work.

1. Totalitarian Regimes of the 20th Century:

By the mid-20th century, totalitarian regimes had taken hold in several parts of the world, most notably under Joseph Stalin in the Soviet Union and Adolf Hitler in Nazi Germany. These regimes were characterized by their control over every aspect of citizens' lives, their use of propaganda, censorship, and the eradication of individual freedoms. Orwell was deeply disturbed by these developments. He had a firsthand experience of totalitarianism during the Spanish Civil War, and he was also deeply skeptical of Stalin's Soviet Union. The mechanisms of control, surveillance, and oppression present in "1984" were very much influenced by Orwell's observations of these regimes.

2. Orwell's Personal Experiences:

George Orwell (the pen name for Eric Arthur Blair) was a committed socialist, but he harbored a deep skepticism of concentrated power, regardless of its ideological orientation. His experiences during the Spanish Civil War (1936-1939) had a profound effect on him. He witnessed the betrayal of the leftist POUM militia (to which he was attached) by the more dominant Stalinist Communists. This betrayal, coupled with the purges and show trials in the USSR, led him to become very wary of the potential dangers of ideological extremism.

3. The Post-War Climate:

World War II reshaped the global political landscape. By its end, two superpowers emerged: the United States and the Soviet Union. The world quickly polarized into Eastern and Western Blocs, leading to the onset of the Cold War. This geopolitical rivalry was characterized by espionage, propaganda, and proxy wars. Orwell's depiction of a world divided into three superstates—Oceania, Eurasia, and Eastasia—reflects this tripartite division and the constant shifting of alliances, reminiscent of the geopolitical fluidity of his time.

4. The Rise of Technology:

The early 20th century saw rapid advancements in technology, especially in mass communication. Radio and film, for example, became powerful tools for propaganda. Orwell extrapolated from this, imagining a future where technology is used not just for propaganda, but for surveillance and mind control. The omnipresent screens in "1984" that broadcast propaganda while also spying on citizens echo this fear.

5. Linguistic Manipulation:

Orwell, a writer and a linguist at heart, was deeply interested in the relationship between language and thought. The development of "Newspeak" in "1984" reflects his concerns about how language could be used and manipulated by those in power to control thought. This was not just a theoretical concern for Orwell; he had observed how totalitarian regimes altered and twisted language for their purposes.

6. Historical Revisionism:

The novel portrays a regime that constantly alters the past to suit its present objectives. This theme was influenced by Orwell's observations of real-world historical revisionism, particularly in Stalin's USSR, where inconvenient individuals were erased from photographs and history books.

7. Literature and Propaganda:

Literature has often been a platform for critiquing the establishment, but totalitarian regimes often co-opted and weaponized literature and the arts for their purposes. "1984" reflects on this by showing how the ruling Party manipulates literature, art, and even songs. The character of Syme, for instance, who works on the Eleventh Edition of the Newspeak Dictionary, reveals the Party's intent to render any kind of dissenting or free thought impossible by simply eliminating words that can express such ideas.

8. Concept of Doublethink:

A major concept Orwell introduced in "1984" is that of "doublethink" - the capacity to hold two contradictory beliefs simultaneously and accept both of them. It's a cognitive dissonance that allows the Party to rewrite history and assert absolute truths, even if those truths change daily. This concept was a reflection on the absurdities and contradictions Orwell saw in the propaganda of totalitarian states of his time. For example, the Stalinist purges not only physically eliminated opponents but also sought to erase them from historical memory, effectively rewriting the past.

9. Personal Life and Health Influences:

By the time he was writing "1984", Orwell's health was deteriorating, mainly from tuberculosis. This personal suffering and awareness of mortality may have contributed to the bleakness and urgency of the novel. There's a palpable sense of despair and inevitability in "1984", which may be reflective of Orwell's personal struggles at the time.

10. Earlier Works and Continuation of Themes:

It's also worth noting that "1984" wasn't Orwell's first critique of totalitarianism. His 1945 novella "Animal Farm" is a satirical allegory of the Russian Revolution and its aftermath, specifically the rise of Stalinism. Some of the themes he touched upon in "Animal Farm", such as the corrupting influence of power and the betrayal of revolutionary ideals, find deeper exploration in "1984".

11. The Role of Media:

Orwell was deeply concerned about the manipulative power of media. In the novel, the state-controlled media disseminates propaganda, alters news, and revises history, all to fit the Party's narrative. This concern can be traced back to Orwell's observations of how media was used during his time, whether it was the state-controlled media in totalitarian regimes or even the more subtle biases in the free-world press.

12. Loss of Individualism:

Central to "1984" is the theme of the loss of individualism in the face of state machinery. Characters such as Winston and Julia seek personal freedom and intimacy in a world where such concepts are alien. Their rebellion, their love, and their quest for truth are all set against a backdrop of a society that seeks to suppress individual desires and aspirations. This can be seen as a reflection of Orwell's broader concerns about the individual's place in a rapidly modernizing and bureaucratizing world.

13. The Influence of World Wars:

The two World Wars had a profound effect on the collective psyche of the nations involved. The devastation, loss, and upheaval shook the foundational beliefs of many. The wars also gave rise to technologies and systems of surveillance and control. In "1984", the perpetual state of war and the manner in which war is used by the Party to control and manipulate the masses can be traced back to Orwell's contemplations on the lasting impacts of World Wars on society.

14. Psychological Manipulation:

The Party doesn't just control through force; it employs profound psychological manipulation. The torture of Winston isn't just physical; it's deeply psychological, aimed at breaking his spirit and realigning his beliefs. This speaks to Orwell's understanding of the human psyche and how totalitarian regimes don't just want obedience, they want belief and complete ideological submission.

15. Influence of Dystopian Predecessors:

Orwell's "1984" did not emerge in a vacuum. Dystopian literature, with authors like Aldous Huxley and his "Brave New World" or Yevgeny Zamyatin's "We", explored the dangers of unchecked technological advancement and the loss of individuality. Orwell's work can be seen in conversation with these novels, presenting a different facet of a dystopian future.

16. Philosophical Underpinnings:

Philosophically, Orwell grapples with relativism in "1984". The Party's assertion that reality is what it says it is, and its ability to shape truth, poses deep philosophical questions. If an entity can control memory, perception, and recorded history, can it also control reality? This exploration of the nature of truth, reality, and belief has roots in philosophical debates that date back centuries.

17. Love and Human Connection:

Amidst the bleakness, the relationship between Winston and Julia offers a glimmer of hope. It underscores the human need for connection, intimacy, and love. Even in the direst circumstances, human beings seek out such connections, making it an act of resistance in itself. Orwell seems to suggest that the personal is indeed political.

18. Parallels with Contemporary Society:

While "1984" was written as a warning, Orwell might have seen the seeds of such a society in his time. The rise of mass media, the beginnings of computer technology, and centralized governmental control over many aspects of life in war-time Britain might have given him glimpses of the dangers inherent in these technologies and systems if left unchecked.

19. Reflection on Imperfect Revolutions:

Orwell's other writings, most notably "Animal Farm", reflect on the trajectory of revolutions. "1984" can be seen as a continuation of this thought, pondering what happens when a revolutionary regime, initially promising equity and justice, becomes as corrupt, if not more so, than its predecessor.

20. The Role of Class:

The stratification in "1984", with the Inner Party, Outer Party, and the Proles, reflects Orwell's thoughts on class and hierarchy. Despite revolutionary rhetoric, class distinctions remain, and power dynamics persist. This may have been influenced by Orwell's observations of class structures in Britain and elsewhere.

In conclusion, "1984" is a rich tapestry of ideas, concerns, and reflections, masterfully woven together by George Orwell. His keen insights into human nature, society, and politics, combined with his deep understanding of history and his vision of potential futures, make the novel not just a dystopian narrative but also a profound philosophical exploration of power, truth, and human resilience.

ABOUT GEORGE ORWELL

Early Life and Personal Background:

George Orwell, born Eric Arthur Blair on June 25, 1903, in Motihari, Bihar, British India, was the son of a British colonial civil servant. His early life was marked by a juxtaposition of circumstances: born into the British Raj's colonial setting, yet raised in England, he found himself straddling two worlds. This duality, the outsider's perspective, would prove influential throughout his writing career.

Education:

Orwell was educated at some of England's most prestigious institutions. He attended the preparatory St. Cyprian's School in Eastbourne, Sussex, where he developed an early aversion to the English class system. This distaste was further cultivated at Eton College, where he was surrounded by the future elite of British society. Though a diligent student, Orwell always felt somewhat removed, an observer of the machinations of the upper echelons.

Early Adulthood:

Rejecting the trajectory expected of an Eton alumnus, Orwell chose not to attend university but instead joined the Indian Imperial Police in Burma in 1922. This experience further solidified his anti-imperialist views. He grew increasingly disillusioned with British imperialism and, in 1927, made the significant decision to resign.

Upon his return to England, Orwell dabbled in various vocations, from teaching to bookstore clerking, but it was his experiences of poverty while living in London and Paris that had a profound influence on him. These encounters formed the basis of his work "Down and Out in Paris and London" (1933), which was a gritty, firsthand account of the underbelly of urban life in the two cities.

Family Life:

George Orwell was married twice in his life:

1. Eileen O'Shaughnessy: Orwell met Eileen Maud O'Shaughnessy in 1935, and they married on June 9, 1936. Eileen was a significant influence on Orwell's life, providing both emotional and intellectual support. The couple adopted a son, Richard Horatio Blair, in 1944. Tragically, Eileen died unexpectedly in 1945 during an operation to remove a tumor. Her death deeply affected Orwell, and he often expressed his grief and guilt in his personal writings.

2. Sonia Brownell: Shortly before his death, Orwell married Sonia Brownell in October 1949. They had known each other for several years, and Sonia was with Orwell during the final stages of his illness. After Orwell's death in 1950, Sonia became the executor of his estate and played a pivotal role in managing his posthumous publications and preserving his legacy. The two had a close but complex relationship, with some of Orwell's friends noting Sonia's dedication to him during his illness, while others criticized her for her handling of his estate.

While Eileen and Sonia played different roles in Orwell's life, both women were instrumental in shaping his personal and literary journey.

War and Political Evolution:

Orwell's political convictions were deeply influenced by the tumultuous events of the 1930s and 1940s. During the Spanish Civil War, he fought for the Republicans against Franco's Nationalists and was injured in combat. This period was pivotal; he witnessed firsthand the betrayals and infighting among leftist factions, which informed his growing disdain for totalitarianism on both the political left and right. His experiences in Spain were vividly detailed in "Homage to Catalonia" (1938).

Major Works and Themes:

Two of Orwell's most acclaimed works are "Animal Farm" (1945) and "1984" (1949). Both novels are scathing critiques of totalitarianism. "Animal Farm" uses allegory to depict the Russian Revolution and the subsequent rise of Stalinism, while "1984" paints a chilling portrait of a dystopian future marked by omnipresent surveillance, thought control, and state oppression.

Orwell's writings always exhibited a blend of sharp observation, wit, and a profound sense of justice. He was deeply concerned about the misuse of power, the distortions of truth, and the manipulation of the masses. Language and its potential for both clarity and obfuscation were recurrent themes in his essays, most notably in "Politics and the English Language."

Later Life and Legacy:

Throughout the 1940s, while Orwell's literary reputation grew, his health deteriorated. Tuberculosis, with which he had struggled intermittently, became more pronounced. Despite his ailments, he continued to write, producing some of his most enduring work during this period.

On January 21, 1950, George Orwell passed away in London at the age of 46. Though his life was tragically short, his literary and journalistic contributions left an indelible mark on literature and political thought. Today, Orwell's legacy is that of a fierce critic of totalitarianism, a champion of clarity in language, and a relentless seeker of truth in an age of propaganda and political machination.

His name has even given rise to the adjective "Orwellian," describing a situation, idea, or societal condition that Orwell identified as being destructive to the welfare of a free and open society. It particularly denotes an attitude and a policy of control by propaganda, surveillance, misinformation, denial of truth, and manipulation of the past.

Locations in the novel

The novel "1984" by George Orwell is set in a dystopian future version of Great Britain. The locations and settings in the novel are:

1. Airstrip One: The story primarily unfolds in Airstrip One, which is the new name for the territory that was once known as England. Airstrip One is one of the main provinces of the superstate Oceania.

2. Oceania: This is the superstate in which Airstrip One is located. Oceania is one of the three intercontinental superstates that divide the world among themselves. The other two superstates are Eurasia and Eastasia. Oceania is under the dictatorial rule of the Party led by the enigmatic figure known as Big Brother.

3. The City of London: Much of the action in the novel takes place in a grim, deteriorated version of London, which is the chief city of Airstrip One. It is here that the protagonist, Winston Smith, lives and works. The city is characterized by dilapidated buildings, invasive telescreens, and omnipresent surveillance.

4. The Ministry of Truth (Minitrue): This is Winston's workplace, where he alters historical records to fit the Party's current version of events. The building is massive and imposing, adorned with the Party slogans: "WAR IS PEACE," "FREEDOM IS SLAVERY," and "IGNORANCE IS STRENGTH."

5. The Proles' Neighborhood: These are the more impoverished areas where the non-Party members, or "proles," live. The Party largely ignores them, believing them to be inferior and incapable of rebellion.

6. The Ministry of Love (Miniluv): A place associated with fear and torture, it is the center of the Party's operations to suppress dissent and thoughtcrime. Despite its name, it is the most dreaded place in Oceania.

7. Mr. Charrington's Shop: An old shop in the Proles' district where Winston rents a room to secretly meet with Julia, his lover. The shop and the rented room play crucial roles in the plot's development.

8. The Chestnut Tree Café: A significant location in the latter part of the novel, this café is where certain characters are seen after they have been released from the Ministry of Love, and it serves as a symbol of resignation and defeat.

The settings in "1984" are dreary, reflecting the oppressive nature of the Party's rule and the bleakness of the dystopian society that Orwell envisioned. The landscape is marked by decay, constant surveillance, and an omnipresent sense of fear.

CONTEXT, PROCESS, AND INSPIRATIONS BEHIND THE NOVEL

"1984" by George Orwell was written as a novel. Here's a detailed exploration:

1. Historical and Political Context:
The backdrop for the creation of "1984" was the mid-20th century, a time rife with political upheaval, the rise of totalitarian regimes, and the aftermath of World War II. Orwell was deeply affected by the global political landscape, especially the rise of Stalinism in the Soviet Union and the spread of fascism in Europe.

2. Personal Experience:
Orwell's personal experiences, particularly during the Spanish Civil War, where he witnessed the betrayals and infighting among leftist factions, deeply influenced his perspective on totalitarianism and ideological purity.

3. Writing Process:
Orwell began writing "1984" around 1947, and it was published in 1949. He wrote the novel on the Scottish island of Jura, where he moved in 1946. The environment was remote, and Orwell, who was battling tuberculosis, often worked under challenging conditions. The sense of isolation and introspection, coupled with his deteriorating health, might have contributed to the novel's bleak tone.

4. Influence of Earlier Dystopias:
Orwell was undoubtedly influenced by earlier dystopian works, most no-

tably "We" by Yevgeny Zamyatin and "Brave New World" by Aldous Huxley. While "1984" shares thematic concerns with these novels, Orwell's approach is distinctively his own, emphasizing political control and the manipulation of truth.

5. Literary Technique:

Orwell employed a third-person limited perspective in "1984," primarily following the thoughts, experiences, and emotions of the protagonist, Winston Smith. This choice allows readers to intimately understand the Party's oppressive nature and the psychological effects of living under such a regime.

6. Exploration of Language:

Orwell delved deep into the manipulation of language as a means of control in "1984." The invention of "Newspeak," a language designed to eliminate unorthodox thoughts, is a central theme. Orwell's focus on language was not just a literary device but a commentary on how language can be used and misused in political contexts. His essay "Politics and the English Language" can be seen as a companion piece to "1984" in its exploration of this theme.

7. Reception:

Upon its release, "1984" was both lauded and criticized. While many praised its boldness and its warning against totalitarianism, others felt it was overly pessimistic or ideologically biased. However, over time, it has become a canonical work in the dystopian genre and is recognized for its profound insights into politics, power, and human nature.

In essence, "1984" was written as a cautionary tale, warning against the dangers of absolute power and the erosion of individual freedoms. Through its detailed world-building, character development, and exploration of themes like reality, truth, and memory, the novel paints a harrowing picture of a society where the individual is subsumed entirely by the state.

WHY STUDENTS STUDY 1984

"1984" by George Orwell is a staple in many educational curricula around the world due to its rich thematic content, historical significance, and literary merit. Here's a detailed look at why students study "1984":

1. Exploration of Totalitarianism:

One of the primary themes of "1984" is the dangers of totalitarianism. Through the depiction of the Party's absolute control over Oceania's citizens, the novel provides a cautionary tale about the consequences of unchecked power. Studying "1984" allows students to analyze and understand the mechanisms through which totalitarian regimes operate and maintain control.

2. Examination of Language and Thought Control:

The novel delves deep into the manipulation of language as a means of control, particularly through the invention of "Newspeak." This exploration fosters discussions about how language shapes thought and how controlling language can limit the range of human thought and expression.

3. Relevance to Modern Surveillance Societies:

With the advent of modern technology, issues of surveillance, data privacy, and individual rights have become increasingly relevant. "1984" provides a lens through which students can discuss and analyze current events and the potential dangers of a surveillance state.

4. Insight into Propaganda and Manipulation:

The Party's use of propaganda, the rewriting of history, and the manipulation of facts in "1984" offer students an opportunity to study how information can be used as a tool of control. In an era of "fake news" and information overload, these themes are especially pertinent.

5. Study of Individual vs. Collective Identity:

Through Winston's journey, the novel delves into the conflict between individual identity and collective conformity. This exploration promotes discussions about personal freedom, autonomy, and the role of the individual in society.

6. Literary Merit:

"1984" is not only thematically rich but also a work of considerable literary merit. Its narrative structure, character development, and use of symbolism offer students a chance to hone their analytical and critical reading skills.

7. Historical and Political Context:

The novel allows students to explore the historical and political contexts of the mid-20th century, including the rise of totalitarian regimes and the political anxieties of the post-war era. This can lead to broader discussions about history, politics, and the cyclical nature of societal concerns.

8. Ethical and Philosophical Discussions:

The moral and philosophical dilemmas presented in "1984" – such as the nature of reality, the malleability of truth, and the ethics of resistance – provide rich material for debate and reflection.

9. Cultural Impact:

Since its publication, "1984" has had a profound impact on popular culture, giving rise to terms like "Orwellian" to describe situations reminiscent of the novel's dystopian world. Studying "1984" allows students to understand these cultural references and the novel's enduring influence.

In essence, "1984" is a diverse work that provides a wealth of material for academic exploration, critical thinking, and discussion, making it a valuable addition to educational curricula across disciplines and age groups.

EXPLORATION OF TOTALITARIANISM

The exploration of totalitarianism in "1984" is one of its central themes, providing a harrowing portrayal of a society where the state exerts absolute power over every facet of human existence. Let's take a deep look into this theme:

1. Ubiquitous Surveillance:

The iconic image from "1984" is that of Big Brother's eyes, omnipresent and always watching. The slogan "Big Brother is watching you" epitomizes the surveillance state. Telescreens, hidden microphones, and spies are everywhere, ensuring that every citizen is perpetually under observation. This constant monitoring creates an atmosphere of paranoia and fear, a classic tactic of totalitarian regimes to suppress dissent and maintain control.

2. Historical Revisionism:

The Party constantly alters historical records to fit its current narrative. Winston Smith's job at the Ministry of Truth involves rewriting past newspaper articles so that they always align with the Party's ever-shifting version of events. By controlling the past, the Party asserts its dominance over reality and truth, ensuring that it remains infallible in the eyes of the populace.

3. Suppression of Individuality:

In Orwell's dystopia, individual desires, thoughts, and emotions are subordinated to the will of the Party. Individuality is seen as a threat, and any deviation from the Party's ideology, termed "thoughtcrime," is swiftly and brutally punished. The suppression extends to personal relationships, as even love and familial bonds are corrupted to serve the Party's ends.

4. The Role of Propaganda:

The Party inundates the populace with propaganda. The three slogans of the Party – "WAR IS PEACE," "FREEDOM IS SLAVERY," and "IGNO-RANCE IS STRENGTH" – are paradoxical statements designed to stifle critical thinking and promote doublethink, the practice of holding two contradictory beliefs simultaneously. The state-controlled media continually spews the Party's version of truth, shaping perceptions and beliefs.

5. Torture and Reeducation:

The Ministry of Love, a misnomer of the highest order, is the institution responsible for torturing and "reeducating" those who defy the Party. Through physical and psychological torture, dissenters like Winston are broken down and reshaped, their rebellious spirits crushed and replaced with absolute loyalty to Big Brother.

6. The Illusion of Opposition:

To maintain control over dissent, the Party creates controlled opposition in the form of the Brotherhood, led by the elusive Emmanuel Goldstein. The daily "Two Minutes Hate" sessions directed against Goldstein serve to channel and manipulate the populace's anger and frustrations, ensuring that it's always directed where the Party desires.

7. Newspeak:

Totalitarianism in "1984" isn't just about overt control but also about subtler forms of manipulation. The development of Newspeak, a language designed to limit the range of thought, is a testament to the Party's intent to eradicate even the possibility of rebellious thoughts. By reducing vocabulary and eliminating "unorthodox" words, the Party aims to make dissent "literally unthinkable."

8. Erasure of Personal History:

Individuals in "1984" have no personal history and no true sense of self outside of their role within the Party. Personal memories that contradict the Party's version of events are dismissed as the result of faulty memory. This erasure of personal history further entrenches the Party's dominance as individuals lose their grounding in their own experiences.

In its depiction of a world dominated by a single, monolithic entity that seeks to control not just actions but thoughts and emotions, "1984" presents a chilling exploration of totalitarianism. The novel serves as a stark warning about the dangers of unchecked power and the lengths to which such regimes will go to maintain their dominance. Through its detailed world-building and character arcs, "1984" offers a profound commentary on the human spirit's resilience and vulnerability in the face of overwhelming oppression.

EXAMINATION OF LANGUAGE AND THOUGHT CONTROL

The relationship between language and thought control is one of the most profound themes in "1984". George Orwell meticulously crafts a narrative that underscores how manipulating language can be a powerful tool for controlling the masses. Here's an in-depth look at this theme:

1. Newspeak:

The most direct representation of language control in "1984" is the invention of Newspeak. This constructed language is designed by the Party to diminish the range of thought. By eliminating words that refer to freedom, rebellion, or individual expression and by simplifying the remaining vocabulary, the Party aims to make any unorthodox thought "literally unthinkable."

2. Doublethink:

Alongside Newspeak is the concept of doublethink, the mental discipline that allows one to believe two contradictory ideas simultaneously. For instance, despite the contradictory nature of the Party's slogans ("WAR IS PEACE," "FREEDOM IS SLAVERY," "IGNORANCE IS STRENGTH"), citizens are conditioned to accept them without question. This manipulation showcases how, by controlling language and the concepts it can express, the Party can shape and limit the very thoughts people have.

3. The Mutability of History:

Winston's job at the Ministry of Truth involves rewriting historical records

rewriting historical records to align with the Party's current stance. By changing the narrative of the past constantly and then insisting that the revised version has always been the truth, the Party uses language as a tool to mold reality. Citizens, constantly bombarded with these "truths," come to distrust their own memories, further cementing the Party's control over their perceptions.

4. The Power of Naming:

Throughout the novel, the names of various ministries illustrate the Party's manipulative use of language. The Ministry of Peace concerns itself with war, the Ministry of Truth with lies, and the Ministry of Love with torture. By co-opting and corrupting the meanings of words, the Party ensures that even the most basic linguistic tools for dissent are rendered impotent.

5. Proles and Oldspeak:

The Proles (proletarians), who constitute the majority of Oceania's population, still speak in Oldspeak (standard English). The Party doesn't feel the need to introduce Newspeak to them because they are considered intellectually inferior and incapable of rebellion. This distinction between the language of the Party members and the Proles highlights how language is tied to power structures and control.

6. Ritualized Hate:

Language is also weaponized in rituals like the "Two Minutes Hate" and "Hate Week." These orchestrated events are filled with charged language designed to stir emotions and direct the populace's anger and fear towards state-sanctioned enemies, further binding them to the Party.

7. The Destruction of Authentic Expression:

In Oceania, authentic personal expression is almost non-existent. The Party suppresses literature, art, and music that could promote individual thought or emotion. Even personal relationships are corrupted by the Party's manipulation of language, as seen in the lack of genuine intimacy between family members and the promotion of "goodsex" (state-approved procreation) over "sexcrime" (intimate relationships based on love or lust).

In "1984", George Orwell presents a chilling vision of how language, when manipulated and restricted by those in power, can be used to limit freedom of thought and solidify control over a populace. The novel serves as a stark reminder of the intrinsic link between language, thought, and freedom, urging readers to be vigilant about any attempts to distort or restrict the words we use and the ideas they represent.

Relevance to modern surveillance societies

"1984" is often hailed as a prophetic work that eerily mirrors certain aspects of contemporary society, especially when it comes to surveillance. The novel's depiction of a society where individuals are constantly monitored serves as a cautionary tale for the modern world, where technological advancements have made pervasive surveillance more feasible than ever. Let's delve into the relevance of "1984" in relation to modern surveillance societies:

1. Omnipresent Surveillance:

In "1984", telescreens are omnipresent in every citizen's home, public spaces, and workplaces, constantly transmitting propaganda while simultaneously monitoring individuals. This omnipresence mirrors today's vast array of surveillance tools – from closed-circuit television (CCTV) cameras in public spaces to digital devices that capture vast amounts of personal data.

2. Digital Footprints:

While Orwell's vision featured physical devices for surveillance, today's reality encompasses digital footprints. Every click, search, purchase, and interaction online leaves a trail. Tech companies, governments, and third-party entities have access to vast amounts of personal data, drawing parallels to the intrusive gaze of Big Brother.

3. State Surveillance:

Many modern governments have established extensive surveillance programs in the name of national security. Revelations about programs like the USA's PRISM or the UK's Tempora, which involve monitoring internet communications at scale, bring to mind the invasive tactics of the Party in Orwell's dystopia.

4. Corporate Surveillance:

In the contemporary era, it's not just governments that partake in surveillance. Corporations, especially tech giants, amass staggering amounts of data on users, often without explicit informed consent. This data is leveraged for targeted advertising, predictive analytics, and sometimes shared with or sold to third parties, further expanding the surveillance net.

5. Chilling Effects on Behavior:

The knowledge (or even the mere perception) of being watched can alter behavior, leading to self-censorship. In "1984", the fear of the Thought Police and the omnipresent telescreens causes citizens to constantly monitor their own behavior and expressions. Similarly, in modern societies, the awareness of surveillance can suppress dissent, limit free expression, and promote conformity.

6. Smart Devices and IoT:

The rise of smart devices, from phones to household appliances connected to the Internet of Things (IoT), expands the surveillance frontier. These devices, while offering convenience, continually collect data, turning homes into potential hubs of personal surveillance reminiscent of the telescreens in the novel.

7. Social Media and Peer Surveillance:

"1984" introduces the idea of peer surveillance, where citizens are encouraged to report on one another. In today's world, social media platforms can sometimes serve a similar function. Public shaming, cancel culture, or even state-sponsored online brigades can monitor, report, and coerce individuals, creating an environment where users police each other.

8. Facial Recognition and Biometric Data:

The Party in "1984" has an uncanny knowledge of every individual's whereabouts and actions. Modern technological advancements in facial recognition and biometric data collection have made this aspect of the novel increasingly relevant, as these tools offer unprecedented abilities to track and identify individuals on a massive scale.

9. Ethical Debates:

"1984" serves as a discussion point in many ethical debates around surveillance. As technology blurs the line between public and private spheres, the novel provides a framework to discuss the balance between security and privacy, the rights of the individual versus the perceived greater good, and the potential consequences of unchecked surveillance.

In summary, while "1984" is a work of fiction, its exploration of surveillance and the erosion of personal privacy resonates deeply with contemporary concerns. The novel stands as a stark reminder of the potential dangers of pervasive surveillance and the importance of safeguarding individual rights and freedoms in an increasingly interconnected digital age.

INSIGHT INTO PROPAGANDA AND MANIPULATION

"1984" is a masterclass in portraying the dark arts of propaganda and manipulation, illustrating how these tools can be used by those in power to shape reality, control perceptions, and maintain an unyielding grip on the populace. Here's a detailed exploration of how the novel delves into these themes:

1. The Role of the Ministry of Truth:

The ironically named Ministry of Truth, where protagonist Winston Smith works, is the epicenter of the Party's propaganda machine. It's here that historical records are altered, newspapers are rewritten, and photographs are doctored to ensure the Party's narrative remains consistent and uncontested. By manipulating the past, the Party controls the present, rendering any dissenting memory a mere "falsehood."

2. Doublethink and Cognitive Dissonance:

The concept of doublethink—holding two contradictory beliefs simultaneously—is central to the Party's manipulation tactics. Citizens are conditioned to accept glaring contradictions without question. This suppression of cognitive dissonance not only halts critical thinking but also forces individuals to accept the Party's version of reality, no matter how illogical.

3. State-sanctioned Hate:

Ritualized expressions of hatred, such as the "Two Minutes Hate" or "Hate Week," serve to channel the populace's emotions and unite them against a common enemy—often the elusive Emmanuel Goldstein. These sessions of directed fury not only divert attention from the Party's failings but also

Party's failings but also create an "us vs. them" mentality, further binding citizens to the Party's cause.

4. Repetition as a Tool:

Repetition is a potent tool in the arsenal of propaganda, and the Party employs it masterfully. From omnipresent slogans like "WAR IS PEACE" and "IGNORANCE IS STRENGTH" to repeated broadcasts about production figures and war victories, the ceaseless repetition aims to engrain the Party's messages into the psyche of every citizen.

5. The Manipulation of Language:

Newspeak, the constructed language of the Party, is a blatant attempt to curtail thought by limiting the words available for expression. By eradicating words related to dissent, freedom, or rebellion and by simplifying the rest, the Party aims to create a language where "thoughtcrime"—unorthodox or rebellious thoughts—is impossible due to a lack of terminology to express it.

6. The Cult of Personality:

The figure of Big Brother, though likely fictional, looms large in the consciousness of Oceania's citizens. His benevolent yet stern visage is omnipresent, creating an illusion of a paternalistic and omniscient leader watching over his subjects. This cult of personality further consolidates the Party's control, as it evokes both adoration and fear.

7. The Suppression of Truth:

In the world of "1984", truth is what the Party deems it to be. Objective reality is dismissed. As O'Brien chillingly puts it to Winston during his interrogation, "Whatever the Party holds to be the truth, is truth." This absolute power over truth allows the Party to manipulate reality at will.

8. Control over Information Flow:

The Party exercises complete control over all mediums of information—be it print, broadcast, or other forms. By controlling what information is disseminated, how it's presented, and even how it's perceived (thanks to doublethink), the Party ensures that citizens are always in a state of controlled awareness, isolated from any facts that might spur dissent.

9. Emotional Manipulation:

Beyond just facts and figures, the Party excels at manipulating emotions. Love and loyalty towards Big Brother, hatred for the enemy, and fear of the Thought Police are all emotions the Party cultivates and controls to maintain its dominance.

In conclusion, "1984" presents a harrowing look into how propaganda and manipulation can be systematically employed to control a society, subjugating its people's minds and emotions. George Orwell's portrayal serves as a timeless warning about the fragility of truth in the face of orchestrated deceit and the importance of critical thinking in resisting manipulation.

STUDY OF INDIVIDUAL VS. COLLECTIVE IDENTITY

"1984" is a profound exploration of the tension between individual identity and collective conformity. At its core, the narrative delves into the crushing weight of a totalitarian regime on the spirit of the individual, examining how identity is shaped, manipulated, and often obliterated for the sake of the collective. Here's a detailed examination of this theme:

1. Suppression of Individuality:

From the onset, the Party's dominance is predicated on the suppression of individual thought and expression. Citizens are discouraged, and often punished, for demonstrating any form of personal autonomy or dissent. This creates a society where individual identity is subsumed by a collective consciousness, defined and dictated by the Party.

2. Uniformity as Control:

The Party enforces a uniform way of life for its members. From the plain blue overalls that Party members wear to the standardization of their routines, there's a deliberate erasure of personal identity. This enforced sameness serves to blur individual lines, ensuring that the collective's needs and beliefs always overshadow personal desires and thoughts.

3. Winston's Struggle for Selfhood:

The protagonist, Winston Smith, embodies the human yearning for selfhood and individual expression. His secret diary becomes a symbol of this desire—a space where he can be true to his thoughts, feelings, and memories. His relationship with Julia also becomes an act of individual rebellion, as they seek moments of personal connection in a world that denies them.

4. Collective Rituals:

Events like the "Two Minutes Hate" and "Hate Week" exemplify how groupthink and collective emotions are harnessed and intensified. These events not only promote a unified hatred towards a common enemy but also suppress individual reasoning and reactions, pushing everyone into a shared frenzied state.

5. The Proles as a Counterpoint:

The Proles (proletarians) offer an interesting contrast to Party members. While they live in poverty and ignorance, they retain certain freedoms—like the ability to express individual emotions, maintain personal relationships, and engage in cultural practices. The Party dismisses the Proles as inconsequential, but their very existence underscores the inherent human need for individual identity.

6. The Role of Memory:

Memory, in "1984", is intrinsically linked to identity. The Party's manipulation of the past, where events are constantly rewritten and individuals "vaporized," highlights their endeavor to control personal and collective memory. By doing so, they aim to control individual identities, ensuring that citizens' understanding of themselves aligns with the Party's narrative.

7. O'Brien and Collective Allegiance:

O'Brien's interactions with Winston provide insight into the Party's philosophy regarding individuality. To O'Brien, and by extension the Party, individual thought or rebellion is a temporary anomaly—a "fault in the pattern" that must be rectified. Their goal is a society where individual consciousness is entirely merged with the Party's will.

8. The Crushing of Winston's Identity:

Winston's eventual breakdown in the Ministry of Love is not just physical torture but a systematic dismantling of his individual identity. His memories, beliefs, and emotions are torn apart until he can genuinely declare his love for Big Brother, signaling the final surrender of his individual self to the collective.

9. The Illusion of Individual Rebellion:

Throughout the novel, avenues that appear to offer individual rebellion, like the Brotherhood or Goldstein's book, are revealed to be under the Party's control or fabrication. This serves as a bleak commentary on the near-impossibility of genuine individual resistance in the face of overwhelming collective control.

In conclusion, "1984" is a chilling portrayal of the conflict between individual identity and collective conformity. Through its characters, events, and settings, the novel delves into the lengths to which a totalitarian regime will go to erase individuality, highlighting the inherent human struggle to maintain a sense of self in the face of such oppression.

LITERARY MERIT

George Orwell's "1984" is more than just a dystopian novel; it's a work of literary significance that has carved its place in the annals of classic literature. Its literary merit can be examined from multiple facets, all of which underscore its enduring relevance and craftsmanship:

1. Masterful World-building:

Orwell paints a vivid and terrifying picture of the world of Oceania. From the grimy streets of Airstrip One to the towering, imposing structure of the Ministry of Truth, the setting is meticulously crafted. The details, like the omnipresent telescreens and the drab uniformity of Party members' lives, immerse readers into a bleak world of totalitarian control.

2. Innovative Use of Language:

The invention of "Newspeak" is a stroke of literary genius. It's not just a fictional language but a crucial tool used by the Party to control and limit thought. Phrases like "doublethink" and "thoughtcrime" and the truncation and amalgamation of words in Newspeak reflect the Party's desire to constrain language and, by extension, thought.

3. Profound Themes:

"1984" delves deep into themes of freedom, identity, truth, and the nature of power. Orwell's examination of how truth can be manipulated, how individuality can be crushed, and how freedom can be redefined is both thought-provoking and disturbing.

4. Complex Characters:

Winston, with his frailties, fears, and moments of defiance, is a compelling

iance, is a compelling protagonist. He embodies the human spirit's struggle against oppressive forces. Characters like Julia, O'Brien, and even Big Brother himself (or the idea of him) are intricately layered, showcasing various facets of conformity, rebellion, and power.

5. Narrative Structure:

Orwell employs a third-person limited perspective, closely following Winston's experiences. This choice provides readers with an intimate understanding of Winston's thoughts and emotions, making his journey and eventual tragedy deeply personal.

6. Allegorical Elements:

Many elements in "1984" are allegorical, representing broader societal and political phenomena. The ever-watchful Big Brother can be seen as a symbol of invasive state control, while the proles represent the oft-ignored masses who, despite their numbers, remain powerless.

7. Philosophical Dialogues:

Scattered throughout the novel are profound dialogues and monologues, especially during Winston's interactions with O'Brien. These discussions challenge perceptions of reality, truth, and the nature of power, pushing readers to ponder these concepts deeply.

8. Impact on Popular Culture:

The sheer influence of "1984" on popular culture is a testament to its literary merit. Terms like "Orwellian" have entered everyday lexicons, indicating situations reminiscent of the novel's oppressive regime. The concept of "Big Brother" has been used in various contexts, from reality TV shows to discussions on surveillance.

9. Enduring Relevance:

A significant marker of literary merit is timelessness, and "1984" possesses this quality in spades. Despite being written in the mid-20th century, its themes resonate in contemporary discussions on privacy, surveillance, misinformation, and governmental control.

10. Moral and Ethical Provocations:

"1984" isn't just a novel; it's a moral and ethical examination. It challenges readers to consider the fragility of freedom, the importance of truth, and the depths to which humanity can sink in the quest for absolute power.

In conclusion, the literary merit of "1984" lies in its intricate blend of storytelling, character development, thematic depth, and socio-political commentary. Its ability to engage, challenge, and disturb readers ensures its place as a cornerstone of modern literature, continuing to inspire debates and reflections even decades after its publication.

HISTORICAL AND POLITICAL CONTEXT

"1984" cannot be fully appreciated without understanding the historical and political milieu in which George Orwell wrote. The novel, though futuristic in its setting, is deeply rooted in the socio-political concerns of the mid-20th century. Here's a detailed dive into the historical and political context that influenced "1984":

1. The Shadow of Totalitarianism:

By the time Orwell began writing "1984" in the late 1940s, the world had witnessed the rise and consolidation of totalitarian regimes in Nazi Germany and Stalinist Soviet Union. These regimes, with their massive propaganda machines, cults of personality, and ruthless suppression of dissent, served as real-life templates for the fictional totalitarian state of Oceania.

2. World War II's Aftermath:

The world had just emerged from the devastating World War II, witnessing unprecedented destruction and the realignment of global powers. The wartime alliance between the Western nations and the Soviet Union was unraveling, giving way to the Cold War. The omnipresent state of war in "1984", where alliances shift and enemies change, mirrors the geopolitical uncertainties of Orwell's time.

3. The Cold War and the Bipolar World:

Post-World War II, the world was increasingly polarized between the capitalist West, led by the United States, and the communist East, led by the Soviet Union. This bipolar world, characterized by ideological conflict, es-

aracterized by ideological conflict, espionage, and the threat of nuclear annihilation, finds echoes in the novel's three superstates: Oceania, Eurasia, and Eastasia.

4. Stalinist Purges and Propaganda:

Orwell was deeply disturbed by the purges, show trials, and the rewriting of history in the Soviet Union under Stalin. The character of Big Brother shares parallels with Stalin, while the practices of the Party in altering history and erasing individuals from existence are reminiscent of Stalinist tactics.

5. Spanish Civil War and Orwell's Disillusionment:

Orwell's personal experiences during the Spanish Civil War, where he fought against Franco's fascists, deeply influenced his political outlook. He witnessed firsthand the betrayals and infighting among leftist factions and the role of propaganda. These experiences, particularly his disenchantment with Soviet-backed communists, informed much of the political cynicism in "1984".

6. Rise of Mass Media and Propaganda:

The 20th century saw the rapid proliferation of mass media, especially radio and film. While these were tools of entertainment and information, they were also harnessed for propaganda by totalitarian regimes. The omnipresent telescreens in "1984" that broadcast Party propaganda and double as surveillance devices reflect these developments.

7. Post-war Surveillance States:

In the aftermath of World War II, both the East and West established extensive intelligence and surveillance networks driven by Cold War paranoia. While the extent of surveillance in "1984" is hyperbolic, it draws from the real-world expansion of state surveillance during Orwell's lifetime.

8. Fear of Technological Misuse:

The 20th century was a period of rapid technological advancement. While these developments promised progress, there was also growing apprehension about technology's misuse, especially in the hands of oppressive governments. "1984" explores these fears, depicting a world where technology is employed not to better human lives but to monitor and control them.

9. Existential and Philosophical Concerns:

Beyond political events, the early to mid-20th century was a period of deep existential and philosophical introspection, influenced by two World Wars and the realization of humanity's capacity for self-destruction. "1984" taps into these existential anxieties, questioning the nature of truth, reality, and human freedom.

In essence, "1984" is a product of its time, encapsulating the fears, anxieties, and political observations of a world that had witnessed unprecedented conflict, the rise of powerful ideologies, and the potential for both technological marvel and misuse. Orwell's work stands as a cautionary tale, drawing from the tapestry of his contemporary world to warn future generations of the perils of unchecked power and the fragility of freedom.

ETHICAL AND PHILOSOPHICAL DISCUSSIONS

"1984" by George Orwell is a treasure trove of ethical and philosophical musings, many of which continue to resonate with readers today. The novel beckons its audience to grapple with profound questions about truth, freedom, reality, and the human spirit. Here's a detailed exploration of the ethical and philosophical discussions embedded within the fabric of the novel:

1. The Nature of Truth:

"1984" dives deep into the malleability of truth in the hands of those in power. The Party's slogan, "Who controls the past controls the future; who controls the present controls the past," speaks to the terrifying ability of the regime to redefine reality. It prompts readers to question: Is truth absolute, or can it be reshaped and repackaged?

2. Doublethink and Cognitive Dissonance:

The concept of "doublethink" — holding two contradictory beliefs simultaneously — is a philosophical conundrum. It confronts the idea of cognitive dissonance and the human capacity to accommodate conflicting realities, especially under duress or indoctrination.

3. Freedom and Slavery:

The Party's disturbing proclamation, "Freedom is Slavery," challenges conventional understandings of freedom. Is absolute freedom, without societal structures or constraints, a form of anarchy or even self-destruction? Conversely, can security or unity, even under an oppressive regime, be a form of liberation for some?

4. The Essence of Humanity:

Through Winston's struggles and the broader societal landscape, the novel examines what it means to be human. Is it our memories, our emotions, our capacity for love? Or is it our ability to think freely and critically? And can the essence of humanity be extinguished by an oppressive system?

5. The Power of Language:

The novel's exploration of "Newspeak" touches on the philosophy of language. It raises questions about how language shapes thought and reality. If words for dissent or rebellion are eliminated, do the concepts themselves vanish?

6. The Individual vs. The Collective:

At its core, "1984" grapples with the tension between individual desires and collective needs. It raises questions about the ethics of sacrificing individual freedoms for the perceived greater good and whether a society can truly prosper by suppressing individuality.

7. Reality, Perception, and Sanity:

Winston's torturous reeducation at the hands of O'Brien challenges the nature of reality. O'Brien's assertion that reality exists in the mind and can be shaped by those in power leads to unsettling philosophical questions about perception, objective reality, and the nature of sanity.

8. The Morality of Rebellion:

Winston and Julia's clandestine relationship, and their association with the supposed Brotherhood, delves into the ethics of rebellion. When is rebellion a moral imperative? And can small acts of personal defiance, even if they achieve no broad change, hold intrinsic value?

9. The Ethics of Surveillance:

With its omnipresent telescreens and the specter of Big Brother, the novel instigates discussions on the morality of surveillance. In an age where technology increasingly blurs the lines between privacy and security, the book's portrayal of invasive monitoring feels eerily prescient.

10. Love, Loyalty, and Betrayal:

The novel's climax, where love and torture intersect in Room 101, forces readers to ponder the limits of human loyalty and the fragility of love under extreme duress. It raises unsettling questions about the moral boundaries one might breach to escape pain.

In weaving these philosophical and ethical threads, "1984" stands as a testament to Orwell's genius. The novel serves not merely as a narrative but as a profound reflection on the human condition, societal structures, and the ethical dilemmas that arise when power goes unchecked. Readers are not just entertained but are compelled to question, think, and engage with the weighty issues presented — a hallmark of truly great literature.

Cultural impact

"1984" by George Orwell isn't just a literary masterpiece; it has permeated deep into cultural consciousness, leaving an indelible mark. This dystopian novel, with its bleak portrayal of totalitarian rule and the erosion of individual freedoms, has influenced art, politics, technology, and public discourse in myriad ways. Delving into its vast cultural impact reveals the following:

1. Introduction of New Vocabulary:
Terms like "Big Brother," "thoughtcrime," "doublethink," and "Newspeak" have transcended the book's pages, becoming integral parts of the modern lexicon. They're used to describe invasive surveillance, cognitive dissonance, linguistic manipulation, and even subtle forms of political or corporate control.

2. Political Discourse:
"Orwellian" has become a byword for any governmental or institutional action that seems to infringe upon individual freedoms or distort truth. Politicians, activists, and commentators worldwide invoke "1984" when discussing policies or actions that hint at surveillance, censorship, or misinformation.

3. Artistic Interpretations:
The novel has inspired countless adaptations across various mediums. From stage productions and films to television series and radio dramas, "1984" has been reimagined multiple times, each interpretation reflecting the specific socio-political concerns of its era.

4. Music and Pop Culture:

Musicians like David Bowie, Radiohead, and The Eurythmics have drawn inspiration from "1984," crafting songs or entire albums influenced by its themes. References to the novel appear in TV shows, comics, and other popular media, attesting to its pervasive cultural resonance.

5. Reflection in Technology and Privacy Debates:

With the advent of modern surveillance technologies, data mining, and AI-driven algorithms, discussions about privacy and control often invoke "1984." The telescreens of the novel find echoes in contemporary debates about smart devices, facial recognition, and the role of tech giants in collecting and leveraging personal data.

6. Educational Impact:

"1984" has become a staple in academic curricula worldwide. Students study the novel not just for its literary merit but also as a cautionary exploration of power dynamics, individual freedoms, and the role of truth in society.

7. Influence on Other Literature:

Orwell's portrayal of a dystopian society has paved the way for other dystopian works, from Aldous Huxley's "Brave New World" to more contemporary offerings like Suzanne Collins' "The Hunger Games" and Margaret Atwood's "The Handmaid's Tale."

8. Social Movements and Activism:

Protesters, from those rallying against autocratic regimes to those advocating for digital privacy, have used imagery and slogans from "1984" to drive home their messages. The iconic image of Big Brother or the phrase "Big Brother is watching you" has been employed in rallies and campaigns across the globe.

9. Philosophical and Ethical Debates:

Beyond its political implications, "1984" has fostered numerous discussions in philosophical and ethical circles. Its exploration of truth, reality, freedom, and human nature has made it a reference point in academic and intellectual debates.

10. Cultural Renewal and Relevance:

The novel's cultural impact isn't static. With changing global dynamics, new technological advancements, and evolving political landscapes, "1984" finds renewed relevance. Sales often spike during periods of political upheaval or when public debates about surveillance and privacy intensify.

In summary, "1984" is more than just a work of fiction; it's a cultural phenomenon. Its influence extends far beyond literature, shaping how society perceives, critiques, and responds to issues of power, control, and freedom. Orwell's masterpiece serves as a touchstone, a warning, and a mirror, reflecting the best and worst facets of humanity and the societies we construct.

Summary of Part One

Part One of George Orwell's "1984" sets the bleak and chilling stage of a dystopian world where freedom, privacy, and individuality are under siege.

Chapter 1:

We are introduced to the gray, dreary landscape of Airstrip One (formerly known as London) in the superstate of Oceania. The towering Ministry of Truth, where protagonist Winston Smith works, looms over the city with its striking architecture, embodying the Party's omnipresence. The clock striking thirteen immediately signals to readers that this world operates differently. The omnipotent gaze of Big Brother is felt everywhere, with posters reminding citizens that "BIG BROTHER IS WATCHING YOU."

Chapter 2:

Winston returns to his flat in Victory Mansions, navigating the smell of boiled cabbage and ragged hallways. He's greeted by a blaring telescreen, an instrument of surveillance and propaganda that cannot be turned off. We meet the Parsons family, embodying Party loyalty, particularly the children who are zealous members of the Spies, a youth organization promoting Party doctrine.

Chapter 3:

Winston's disturbing dream of a beautiful countryside and a group of people under threat introduces us to his sense of loss and yearning. We also learn of the haunting refrain, "Oranges and lemons, say the bells of St. Clement's," hinting at remnants of a past now obliterated by the Party.

Chapter 4:

We get a glimpse into Winston's work at the Ministry of Truth, where he alters historical records to fit the Party's ever-changing narrative. It's a world where history is rewritten daily, ensuring the Party is always right.

Chapter 5:

During lunch, we meet Syme, who is working on the Eleventh Edition of the Newspeak Dictionary. He enthusiastically discusses the beauty of Newspeak, a language designed to diminish thought and make dissent impossible. Winston ponders on the inevitable vaporization of Syme due to his intelligence. We also meet Parsons, the embodiment of the ignorant Party loyalist.

Chapter 6:

Winston reflects on a disturbing memory involving a prostitute, highlighting the Party's control over human sexuality and the eradication of genuine intimacy. This suppression of natural human desires creates a society devoid of warmth and connection.

Chapter 7:

Winston muses on the obliteration of the past, realizing the Party's stranglehold on truth and reality. He remembers snippets from his childhood, particularly the disappearance of his parents and sister during the tumultuous times of the Revolution.

Chapter 8:

Wandering through the prole neighborhoods, Winston finds solace in watching the ordinary, impoverished citizens untouched by Party doctrine. He enters an old shop, where he buys a beautiful glass paperweight, an artifact of a bygone era. The shopkeeper introduces him to the rhyme of St. Clement's, further fueling Winston's yearning for the past. The chapter ends with Winston observing a Party rally, where a speaker vehemently shifts enemies mid-sentence, yet the crowd accepts it without question.

Throughout Part One, Orwell paints a picture of a world steeped in fear, surveillance, and manipulation. Every detail, from the stark living conditions to the manipulated language, underscores the Party's total domination over its citizens. This section masterfully sets up the context, characters, and conflicts that will propel the novel forward, making readers question the nature of reality, truth, and freedom.

Summary of Part Two

Part Two of George Orwell's "1984" deepens the narrative, drawing us further into the labyrinthine intricacies of Winston's burgeoning rebellion and his personal relationships.

Chapter 1:
A covert love story begins to bloom in this bleak world. Winston receives a surreptitious note from Julia, a co-worker, simply stating, "I love you." It's a bold, dangerous gesture, an act of rebellion against the Party, which suppresses individual emotions, particularly romantic love.

Chapter 2:
In a hidden nook away from surveillance cameras, the two share a passionate embrace, an act of defiance against the Party's stranglehold. Julia becomes Winston's ally in a personal resistance movement against the Party's inhumanity.

Chapter 3:
The lovers seek refuge in the rented room above Mr. Charrington's shop, a space seemingly untouched by time. Here, surrounded by relics of a forgotten past, their relationship deepens. This room becomes a sanctuary, a bubble of reality and authenticity in an otherwise fabricated world.

Chapter 4:
Winston and Julia discuss their hatred for the Party. Julia is more pragmatic, hating the Party for its intrusions into her personal life, while Winston despises it on more ideological grounds. They acknowledge the risk they're taking but find solace in their shared dissent.

Chapter 5:

We're introduced to O'Brien, a higher-up in the Party who Winston believes might be an ally or even a fellow dissident. Their conversation dances around rebellion, hinting at shared sentiments but always maintaining plausible deniability.

Chapter 6:

The narrative slows down, focusing on the lovers' meetings in their secret hideaway. Their relationship is not just personal; it's a profound act of political dissent. Through their intimacy, they reclaim their humanity from the Party's oppressive grasp.

Chapter 7:

Winston recalls a memory of his family, a time before the Party took control. He painfully remembers leaving his mother and sister during a famine, highlighting the Party's cruel transformation of familial love into something scarce and fearful.

Chapter 8:

Winston and Julia visit O'Brien's luxurious apartment, an oasis of forbidden luxuries. They drink real wine, listen to music, and most daringly, speak openly of rebellion. O'Brien confirms their suspicions: there is an underground movement against the Party, and he is part of it.

Chapter 9:

The horror of the Party's control is further highlighted when Winston reads a forbidden book, given to him by O'Brien. This book, supposedly written by the leader of the opposition, details the mechanisms of the Party's control and its manipulation of society.

Chapter 10:

But their sanctuary is shattered. The room above Mr. Charrington's shop is raided. The beautiful singing of the prole woman is interrupted by the harsh, cold voice from the telescreen. The Thought Police burst in, and the lovers are apprehended. In a cruel twist, Mr. Charrington reveals himself as a member of the Thought Police.

This section of "1984" is a roller-coaster, oscillating between the tender moments of Winston and Julia's love and the looming dread of the Party's omnipresence. Through their relationship, Orwell explores themes of resistance, humanity, and the transformative power of love in the face of oppression. The devastating conclusion of this part underlines the Party's omnipotent reach, hinting at the bleak challenges the protagonists are about to face.

SUMMARY OF PART THREE

Part Three of "1984" plunges the reader into the darkest corners of the dystopian world, portraying the terrifying consequences of defying the Party's iron grip.

Chapter 1:

Winston awakens to find himself in a brightly lit cell at the Ministry of Love, the very heart of the Party's punishment and reconditioning system. The sterile, cold surroundings are punctuated by the distant screams of other detainees. In this grim setting, prisoners are routinely tortured and vaporized.

Chapter 2:

In a chilling reunion, Winston encounters Ampleforth and Parsons, his former colleagues, both arrested for thoughtcrimes (the word used to describe a person's unorthodox political views). The atmosphere is thick with despair as it becomes clear that no one is safe from the Party's reach.

Chapter 3:

Winston's own ordeal intensifies. He is brutally tortured, both physically and psychologically. The pain is unbearable, but more horrifying is the Party's demand for total ideological submission. It's not enough for Winston to obey; he must truly believe in the Party's dogma.

Chapter 4:

O'Brien emerges as Winston's chief tormentor. It's a shocking betrayal, as Winston once saw him as an ally, perhaps even a savior. Through extended h extended sessions of torture and "reeducation," O'Brien breaks down Winston's resistance, reshaping his thoughts and beliefs.

Chapter 5:

Winston's spirit wavers. Amidst the relentless pain and brainwashing, he clings to his love for Julia, hoping it will anchor him. Yet, the Party's machinery of manipulation is insidious, wearing away at his resolve.

Chapter 6:

A moment of hope ignites when Winston overhears a conversation that suggests the proles are finally rising in rebellion. But this glimmer is quickly extinguished when he realizes it's merely another prisoner's delirious rambling.

Chapter 7:

In the face of unrelenting psychological assault, Winston's defenses crumble. O'Brien forces him to confront his deepest fear, using a cage of starving rats. It's a brutal turning point: to save himself, Winston betrays Julia, pleading for her to take his place. In this harrowing moment, the Party's victory is near complete.

Chapter 8:

A broken Winston is released back into society. He's a shell of his former self, having internalized the Party's doctrines. His rebellious spirit is extinguished, replaced with a hollow acceptance.

Chapter 9:

In a poignant twist, Winston encounters Julia. Their once-passionate bond is now cold and distant. Both have betrayed each other, their love effectively destroyed by the Party's machinations.

Chapter 10:

The novel closes with Winston's complete capitulation. He sits in the Chestnut Tree Café, mindlessly scribbling away. The last vestiges of his rebellion are gone. The final, haunting lines reveal Winston's love for Big Brother, symbolizing the totality of the Party's control over the individual.

In Part Three, Orwell presents a harrowing exploration of the depths to which a totalitarian regime will go to maintain control. Through Winston's suffering and eventual submission, the narrative paints a bleak portrait of the human spirit under extreme duress. The novel's conclusion serves as a grim warning about the dangers of unchecked power and the fragility of individual autonomy in the face of oppressive systems.

Themes of the novel

"1984" by George Orwell is a profound and multi-layered work that delves into a myriad of thematic concerns. Here are the most prominent themes:

1. Totalitarianism and Tyranny:

At its core, "1984" stands as a stark warning against the dangers of totalitarianism. The world Orwell crafts is one where the state exercises absolute power and seeks to control every facet of individual life. Big Brother's omnipresent gaze and the Party's relentless pursuit of ideological purity manifest a regime where personal freedoms are obliterated and dissent is ruthlessly crushed.

2. Manipulation of Truth and Reality:

In Oceania, truth is malleable. The Ministry of Truth engages in ceaseless revision of history, ensuring that the Party's version of events is the only one that exists. This manipulation extends to the very perception of reality, epitomized by the Party's chilling slogan: "War is Peace. Freedom is Slavery. Ignorance is Strength." Through this, Orwell illuminates the pernicious ways in which authoritarian regimes can distort and redefine truth to serve their purposes.

3. Surveillance and Paranoia:

In Winston's world, privacy is a relic of the past. The ever-watchful eye of Big Brother, through telescreens and Thought Police, creates an environment of perpetual surveillance. This omnipresent scrutiny instills a profound sense of paranoia and fear, where even the most intimate thoughts (thoughtcrimes) are subject to state intervention.

4. Language and Thought Control:

Newspeak, the official language of Oceania, is not just a linguistic construct but a tool of oppression. By eliminating words and thus the very capacity to harbor dissenting thoughts, the Party aims to enact cognitive control, creating a populace incapable of conceptualizing resistance.

5. Individual vs. Collective Identity:

Winston's journey is one of personal rebellion against a collective behemoth. The Party's assault is not just on freedom of action but on individual identity. By demanding absolute loyalty and love for Big Brother, the regime seeks to subsume the individual into a vast, homogenous collective, erasing personal desires, memories, and identities.

6. The Nature of Reality and Perception:

Throughout the novel, what is real becomes an elusive concept. Whether through the shifting alliances in the perpetual war, the falsification of the past, or the internal betrayals of the heart, Orwell challenges our understanding of objective reality. In a world dominated by the Party's narratives, perception becomes the only truth.

7. Love and Sexuality:

Amidst the bleakness, the relationship between Winston and Julia emerges as a poignant exploration of love and sexuality as acts of resistance. However, even these deeply human emotions are targets for the Party, which seeks to redirect love from individuals to Big Brother and views sexuality as merely a procreative duty.

8. Betrayal:

The theme of betrayal runs deep, from the personal treacheries between characters to the broader betrayals by the Party against its citizens. The climax of Winston's torture, where he betrays Julia to save himself, underscores the devastating emotional and psychological impacts of the Party's tactics.

Here are more themes explored in the novel:

9. Psychological Manipulation:

Beyond physical coercion, the Party exercises an insidious form of psychological control. Through the constant rewriting of history, the populace's memories are repeatedly reset, preventing them from recognizing the Party's inconsistencies. The induced doublethink—holding two contradictory beliefs simultaneously—further muddles their cognitive clarity, making independent thought nearly impossible.

10. Resistance and Rebellion:

Winston's secret acts of defiance, from writing in his diary to his affair with Julia, underscore the human need to resist oppression. However, the novel raises questions about the true nature and efficacy of rebellion when the oppressor is omnipotent.

11. Role of Technology:

Orwell presciently delves into the role of technology as an instrument of state control. Telescreens, microphones, and other surveillance devices enable the Party to monitor every aspect of a citizen's life, illustrating the dangers of unchecked technological advancements in the hands of a tyrannical regime.

12. Disintegration of Family:

The Party aims to erode traditional family bonds and loyalties, promoting allegiance solely to the Party. Children are indoctrinated and encouraged to report their parents for thoughtcrimes, creating an atmosphere of distrust within families.

13. Alienation and Dehumanization:

Under the Party's regime, individuals are stripped of their humanity. The suppression of personal desires, emotions, and memories leads to a profound sense of alienation. This dehumanization ensures that citizens are more manageable and less likely to rebel.

14. Power and Corruption:

Orwell showcases how the unbridled pursuit of power for its own sake corrupts. The Party's actions aren't solely for the greater good but rather to maintain and expand its dominance. As O'Brien states, "Power is not a means; it is an end."

15. The Role of Intellectuals:

Syme, the linguist working on the Newspeak dictionary, represents the intellectuals who, knowingly or unknowingly, aid oppressive regimes. Despite his awareness of the Party's manipulation of language, he remains loyal, demonstrating the dangers of intellectual complacency.

16. Loss and Nostalgia:

Winston's fleeting memories of a time before the Party—of a lost childhood, familial love, and a world without fear—reflect the deep human yearning for a past that is irretrievably lost. These memories become a source of pain and nostalgia in the suffocating present.

17. Fear as a Control Mechanism:

The perpetual state of war, public hangings, and the omnipresent threat of the Thought Police instill a perpetual fear in the citizens, making them more pliable and less likely to challenge the status quo.

18. The Illusion of Knowledge:

The Party controls not just the present but also the past and the future. By claiming to be the sole arbiter of truth and by rewriting history, it creates an illusion of knowledge, where citizens believe what they are told without questioning, leading to a docile and ignorant populace.

Totalitarianism and Tyranny theme

"1984" presents a nightmarish vision of a world under the thumb of absolute authority, where the suffocating grasp of totalitarianism extends its fingers into every facet of human existence. George Orwell paints a chilling tableau of a society where the state isn't just a governing body but an omnipotent deity demanding unwavering devotion.

Oceania's Landscape:

Orwell sets the stage with the bleak, gray streets of Airstrip One (formerly known as London), punctuated by the menacing edifices of the Ministries. The very architecture exudes oppression, with the towering pyramid of the Ministry of Truth dominating the skyline, its facade bearing the unnerving gaze of Big Brother. This omnipresent image serves as a constant reminder of the Party's watchful eyes, from which no citizen can escape.

Big Brother:

An embodiment of the Party's omnipotence, Big Brother is an elusive figure, more deity than man. His omnipresent image on posters, coins, and telescreens stands as a symbol of eternal vigilance and authority. The repeated slogan, "Big Brother is Watching You," encapsulates the Party's ever-present surveillance, ensuring obedience through fear.

The Thought Police:

A sinister arm of the Party's control, the Thought Police serve as the enforcers of ideological purity. No thought is private, no dissent is tolerated. Even harboring rebellious thoughts, termed "thoughtcrimes," can lead to one's disappearance, exemplifying the extremes to which the state will go to ensure mental and emotional compliance.

Eradication of Individuality:

In this dystopia, the individual exists solely to serve the state. Personal desires, memories, and emotions are subversive. The eradication of individual identity is strikingly evident in the uniformity of dress, the communal "Hate Weeks," and the ritualistic Two Minutes Hate sessions where citizens are whipped into a collective frenzy of anger against Oceania's ever-shifting enemies.

History as a Plaything:

The totalitarian regime understands the power of the past in shaping present perceptions. The Ministry of Truth, a grotesque misnomer, systematically revises history, ensuring the Party is always infallible. Past transgressions vanish, heroes become traitors, and truth becomes an ever-mutable concept. This manipulation showcases the lengths to which the Party will go to control not just the present but the very perception of reality.

The Infallibility of the Party:

In Orwell's chilling vision, the Party doesn't merely seek compliance but absolute belief in its dogma. As O'Brien chillingly remarks, "Whatever the Party holds to be the truth is truth." This divine right to shape reality underscores the Party's claim to absolute power.

A World of Perpetual War:

Oceania is constantly at war, cycling between enemies. Whether it's Eastasia or Eurasia, the specific adversary matters little. What's essential is the perpetual state of conflict, keeping citizens in a state of fear, rallying behind the Party for protection, and accepting increased surveillance and control.

In weaving the theme of **Totalitarianism and Tyranny**, Orwell crafts a grim cautionary tale of the dangers of unchecked power. He explores the multifaceted tools of oppression, from psychological manipulation to brutal force, painting a world where freedom is the ultimate subversion and where the human spirit is relentlessly tested against the machine of the state. The novel stands as a dire reminder of the fragility of democracy and the ever-present threat of tyrannical rule.

MANIPULATION OF TRUTH AND REALITY THEME

In the disquieting universe of "1984," the malleability of truth and the molding of reality are wielded as potent weapons by the Party to consolidate its grip on power. George Orwell crafts a world where the delineation between truth and falsehood is not just blurred but obliterated, drawing readers into the depths of a society where reality is constructed and deconstructed at the whims of an authoritarian regime.

The Ministry of Truth:

This monumentally ironic institution stands as the epicenter of the Party's vast machinery of deception. Far from propagating truth, the Ministry engages in the ceaseless rewriting of history. Here, records are altered, newspapers amended, and photographs vanish into memory holes. The past becomes a shifting quagmire, altered to reflect the ever-changing narratives of the Party. Through this, the state ensures its infallibility; if history can be edited, the Party can never be wrong.

Newspeak:

Orwell introduces us to Newspeak, the state-sanctioned language designed to narrow the range of thought. By eliminating words and thus the concepts they represent, Newspeak curtails the very capacity for dissent or subversive thought. Phrases like "doubleplusgood" replace traditional adjectives, reducing nuance and refining thought to fit the Party's ideals. In this linguistic straightjacket, a populace is slowly conditioned to think only what the Party deems acceptable.

Doublethink:

One of the novel's most insidious concepts is doublethink, the mental discipline that allows individuals to accept two contradictory beliefs simultaneously. It's a method of self-deception, ensuring loyalty to the Party even when faced with its blatant lies. This cognitive dissonance, where war becomes peace, freedom is seen as slavery, and ignorance is strength, highlights the terrifying extent to which the Party controls not just external reality but the inner landscapes of human minds.

Perpetual War:

The state of constant warfare serves the Party's interest in multiple ways, one of which is the manipulation of truth. The enemy keeps changing — sometimes it's Eurasia, sometimes Eastasia — but the populace is made to believe that Oceania has always been at war with the current enemy. This fluidity of 'truth' binds the citizens in a shared belief, irrespective of its veracity.

Winston's Work:

Through the lens of Winston Smith, a protagonist working at the Ministry of Truth, Orwell provides a firsthand account of the meticulous manipulation of facts. Winston's daily tasks involve altering records, doctoring photographs, and revising articles to align with the Party's current stance, making dissenters vanish not just from the world but from history itself.

Reality as Defined by the State:

O'Brien, a high-ranking member of the Party and Winston's tormentor, chillingly articulates the Party's perspective on reality: "Whatever the Party holds to be the truth, is truth." This assertion encapsulates the Party's audacious claim over objective reality. If the Party says two plus two equals five, it becomes an accepted fact, underscoring the malleability of truth in this dystopian world.

Orwell's exploration of the **Manipulation of Truth and Reality** in "1984" is a profound meditation on the fragility of truth in the face of overwhelming power. The novel illuminates the pernicious ways in which authoritarian regimes can distort, redefine, and weaponize truth, shaping it into a tool for indoctrination and control. Through this theme, Orwell issues a stark warning about the ease with which reality can be bent and twisted and the dire consequences of relinquishing our hold on objective truth.

SURVEILLANCE AND PARANOIA THEME

In the oppressive world of "1984", the line between public and private doesn't just blur—it's obliterated. George Orwell crafts a dystopia where the omnipresent eye of the Party, symbolized by the haunting visage of Big Brother, peers into the most intimate corners of human existence. The atmosphere is thick with suspicion, mistrust, and the looming dread of being watched, creating a society underpinned by constant anxiety and suppressed dread.

The Telescreens:
One of the most emblematic symbols of the Party's intrusive surveillance system, telescreens are ubiquitous in Oceania. They're not mere passive devices broadcasting propaganda; they're invasive instruments of observation. With their relentless gaze, they watch citizens day and night, their microphones catching even a whisper of dissent. The thought that "Big Brother is Watching You" is not just a slogan—it's an inescapable reality.

The Thought Police:
In a world where thoughts are as scrutinized as actions, the Thought Police are the embodiment of the Party's grip on the psyche of its citizens. With informants everywhere and even children encouraged to report on their parents, they sow seeds of paranoia, making citizens second-guess their every thought and action. The very notion that thinking against the Party (a thoughtcrime) could lead to one's disappearance amplifies the climate of perpetual anxiety.

Public Hangings and Hate Weeks:

These orchestrated events further augment the culture of surveillance. They serve as both a warning and a tool to identify dissenters. The visceral public display of punishment coupled with collective hysteria serves to enforce conformity, and those not visibly conformist are easily spotted and marked.

Distrust Among Citizens:

Trust becomes a luxury few can afford. Friends turn on friends, families are riddled with suspicion, and lovers betray one another. The Party cultivates this environment deliberately, knowing that divided citizens are less likely to unite against a common enemy—the Party itself.

Winston's Paranoia:

Through Winston's experiences, Orwell gives readers a palpable sense of the paranoia permeating daily life. Whether he's seeking a clandestine spot to pen his rebellious thoughts in his diary, or engaging in a forbidden affair with Julia, the fear of being discovered is ever-present. Even the "proles" (proletariat), seemingly free from Party surveillance, are not entirely beyond the reach of the Thought Police.

Charrington and the Hidden Room:

The rented room above Mr. Charrington's shop seems like a haven for Winston and Julia, a place free from the Party's prying eyes. However, this illusion of privacy is shattered when they're arrested there, revealing that even perceived sanctuaries are under surveillance. The eventual revelation of Charrington's true identity is a testament to the depth of the Party's infiltration and the impossibility of escaping its watchful gaze.

O'Brien's Deception:

Winston's trust in O'Brien and his subsequent betrayal encapsulate the profound paranoia of the novel. The fact that someone whom Winston viewed as a fellow dissenter could be an agent of the Party underscores the unreliability of trust and the omnipresence of the surveillance apparatus.

In "1984", the theme of **Surveillance and Paranoia** paints a haunting picture of a society where privacy is extinct and the individual's innermost thoughts are not safe from intrusion. Orwell's masterful narrative serves as a dire warning about the dangers of unchecked power, the erosion of personal freedoms, and the psychological torment of living under constant scrutiny. The novel poses a chilling question: In a world where you're always being watched, can freedom truly exist?

Language and Thought Control theme

In the somber corridors of Orwell's "1984," words are not mere carriers of thought; they're the very crucible in which thought is forged. The Party, acutely aware of the inextricable link between language and thought, meticulously molds and manipulates language to shape and limit human consciousness. Through this control, it doesn't just seek obedience but an absolute dominion over the very essence of human cognition and individuality.

Newspeak:

The quintessential instrument of linguistic control in the novel is Newspeak, a language painstakingly designed by the Party. Its goal? To narrow the boundaries of thought. By reducing vocabulary, eliminating unorthodox words, and stripping remaining words of secondary meanings, Newspeak aims to render certain ideas—especially subversive ones—unthinkable. Phrases like "doubleplusgood" replace a spectrum of descriptive alternatives, compressing the vast expanse of human emotion and thought into a monochromatic tapestry of Party-approved expressions.

Doublethink:

Parallel to Newspeak is the concept of doublethink—the capacity to hold two contradictory beliefs simultaneously and believe both to be true. This mental gymnastics is not just a byproduct but a requirement of the Party's manipulation of truth and reality. It's a testament to the Party's ambition: to control not just external actions but the internal landscape of the mind.

Memory Hole:

The memory holes in the Ministry of Truth, into which inconvenient documents are discarded to be incinerated, symbolize the Party's endeavor to control the past. By erasing records and altering historical documents, the Party ensures that language (and thus memory and reality) remains malleable, bendable to its present needs.

Prohibited Literature:

Books and other forms of literature that do not align with Party ideology are forbidden. This isn't merely to quash dissent but to restrict the range of human thought. By controlling access to diverse ideas, the Party limits the intellectual horizon of its citizens, confining them to a controlled linguistic pasture.

Winston's Job:

As a worker in the Ministry of Truth, Winston's role is to alter past newspaper articles so that they align with the Party's current version of events. This continuous alteration of the past, executed through language, is a vivid demonstration of how the Party manipulates reality and controls thought.

Slogans:

The Party's paradoxical slogans—"War is Peace," "Freedom is Slavery," and "Ignorance is Strength"—are not just propaganda. They are a cognitive assault, forcing citizens to engage in doublethink and accept the illogical as logical. These slogans epitomize the Party's control over truth and its power to dictate reality through language.

Orwell's exploration of **Language and Thought Control** in "1984" is a profound commentary on the inseparable relationship between language, thought, and freedom. It underscores the terrifying possibility of a regime that understands this relationship and exploits it to cement its own power. Through this theme, Orwell alerts us to the fragility of freedom in the face of linguistic manipulation and the dire need to guard the sanctity of language as a vessel of human thought, expression, and identity.

INDIVIDUAL VS. COLLECTIVE IDENTITY THEME

In the bleak, shadow-strewn realm of Orwell's "1984," the boundary between the self and the collective is not just blurred but systematically and ruthlessly eradicated. Orwell paints a world where the vibrant palette of individuality is drained, leaving only the monochrome hue of the Party. Within this theme, Orwell probes the existential battle between personal identity and collective uniformity and how regimes can exploit this tension to tighten their grip on power.

Subjugation of the Individual:

The Party's dominion in Oceania is established not merely through physical control but through the obliteration of personal identity. Citizens are constantly reminded that their lives are subordinate to the will of the Party. Personal desires, dreams, and even thoughts that diverge from the Party's doctrine are seen as treacherous and are systematically purged or punished.

Uniformity and Rituals:

The Party employs various rituals—like the Two Minutes Hate and group exercises—to drown individual thoughts in a sea of collective fervor. These events create a hive mind, where singular voices and identities merge into a unified chorus of Party-sanctioned emotion and thought.

The Role of Family:

Traditional bonds, such as family, which often foster individual identities and loyalties, are subverted. Children are indoctrinated to serve the Party, even if it means betraying their parents. The sanctity of family is sacrificed at the altar of collective allegiance, ensuring the Party's ideologies permeate every facet of life.

Winston's Resistance:

The protagonist, Winston Smith, embodies the flame of individualism flickering in the oppressive darkness of the Party's collectivism. His secret rebellions, be it maintaining a diary or engaging in a forbidden love affair with Julia, are not just acts of dissent but desperate attempts to reclaim his individual identity. Winston's journey represents the human spirit's eternal struggle to preserve its unique essence against overwhelming conformity.

Julia's Individualism:

Julia, unlike Winston, is not overtly political in her rebellion. Instead, she seeks personal pleasures and freedoms, highlighting a different facet of individualism—one that is grounded in personal desires rather than political ideologies.

O'Brien and the Brotherhood:

The elusive Brotherhood, whether real or a fabrication, serves as a beacon of collective resistance against the Party. Yet, as the narrative unfolds, the lines between individual rebellion and collective resistance blur, especially through O'Brien's interactions with Winston, challenging the reader to ponder the nature and cost of true individuality.

The Crushing Conclusion:

The harrowing climax of the novel, where Winston is tortured and brainwashed in the Ministry of Love, is not just a tale of one man's downfall. It's a grim testament to the Party's might in crushing the individual spirit and subsuming it into the collective. Winston's final acceptance of Big Brother is the tragic surrender of individual identity.

Through the theme of **Individual vs. Collective Identity** in "1984", Orwell crafts a cautionary tale about the fragility of personal identity in the face of overpowering collective ideologies. He challenges us to reflect upon the value of individuality in shaping society and to recognize the dangers when it is suppressed or eradicated. The novel serves as a poignant reminder that the battle for individual identity is intrinsic to the human experience and that its preservation is paramount in any society that values freedom and humanity.

The Nature of Reality and Perception
THEME

In the claustrophobic world of "1984," what is real? The lines between objective reality and subjective perception are deliberately smudged, creating a dizzying mirage where the ground constantly shifts beneath one's feet. With meticulous craftsmanship, Orwell depicts a society where the very fabric of reality is malleable, reshaped at the whims of those in power.

The Party's Dictum:
"The Party tells you to reject the evidence of your eyes and ears. It was their final, most essential command." This chilling proclamation encapsulates the Party's audacity in asserting dominion over reality itself. It's not just about obedience but a total subjugation of individual perception to the Party's narrative.

Historical Revisionism:
The Ministry of Truth, with its eerie misnomer, stands as a colossal monument to the Party's manipulation of reality. Here, history isn't just recorded but constantly rewritten. Past events, individuals, and even entire political movements are obliterated or altered, ensuring that the Party is always right, always triumphant. Winston, working within its walls, finds himself ensnared in this grotesque dance, erasing and rewriting facts, making the populace believe in a reality that's been meticulously manufactured.

Memory and Reality:
Without tangible records or consistent narratives, individual memory becomes the sole guardian of reality. Yet, memories, too, are fallible, suscepti-

e fallible, susceptible to doubt, especially when everything and everyone around vehemently denies their veracity. The constant flux of 'truths' forces individuals to rely on the Party for their understanding of reality, making them vulnerable to its manipulations.

Doublethink:

A chilling cognitive mechanism, doublethink allows individuals to accept contradictory beliefs simultaneously. It's the mental contortionism demanded by the Party to align personal perception with its ever-changing narrative. By mastering doublethink, citizens not only accept but also believe the Party's version of reality, however implausible.

Winston's Descent:

Winston's tormenting journey is, at its core, a quest for reality. His clandestine diary, his affair with Julia, and his association with O'Brien are all desperate attempts to touch the bedrock of truth beneath the shifting sands of the Party's lies. The haunting climax in Room 101 is more than physical torture—it's an assault on Winston's perception of reality. His eventual capitulation, symbolized by his betrayal of Julia and acceptance of Big Brother, marks the triumph of a fabricated reality over individual perception.

The Role of Technology:

Telescreens, omnipresent and watchful, not only surveil but also perpetuate the Party's version of reality. By controlling information flow and constantly feeding propaganda, they blur the line between the real and the constructed.

Through the theme of **The Nature of Reality and Perception** in "1984", Orwell offers a harrowing exploration into the fragility of truth in the face of overwhelming power. He compels readers to question the nature of reality, the reliability of their perceptions, and the lengths to which authority can go to manipulate both. It's a stark reminder of the importance of critical thinking, the dangers of blind acceptance, and the profound human need to hold onto an objective sense of reality amidst a sea of deceptions.

Love and Sexuality theme

Within the stifling, oppressive atmosphere of Orwell's "1984", love and sexuality emerge not merely as human instincts but as profound acts of rebellion, threads of human connection that the Party seeks to sever and redefine. The tapestry of this theme is woven with both the tender and the tormenting, revealing the lengths to which an authoritarian regime might go to suppress genuine emotion and connection.

The Party's Manipulation:

The Party's approach to love and sexuality is chillingly clinical. It seeks to drain these deeply personal experiences of all emotion and pleasure, transforming them into mere functional acts for the propagation of the Party's future generations. The sanctity of marital bonds, the thrill of romance, and the intimacy of sexual connection are all treated as potential threats, avenues through which unorthodox thoughts and rebellions might blossom.

Julia and Winston:

In the grey, mechanistic world of Oceania, the clandestine affair between Julia and Winston emerges as a vibrant splash of color, a defiant assertion of individualism and human connection. Their physical intimacy becomes an act of political defiance, a space where they reclaim their bodies and minds from the Party's clutches. However, it's not just the act, but the emotions, the shared moments of vulnerability and trust, that make their relationship a beacon of hope and resistance.

Julia's Perspective:

Julia's approach to sexuality is intrinsically rebellious. For her, it's an expression of personal freedom, a way to snatch a piece of individuality from under the Party's gaze. She has had multiple affairs with Party members, each act serving as a quiet defiance against the system's sterile, emotionless approach to sexuality.

Sexual Orthodoxy:

The Party promotes the "Anti-Sex League" and instills in its members a kind of repulsion for the act, save for procreation. By doing so, it not only controls the physical act but also seeks to kill the deeper emotional connections that can arise from it. In essence, the Party aims to make sexual relationships devoid of passion, turning them into mere transactions.

The Ultimate Betrayal:

One of the most heart-wrenching moments in the novel is Winston's betrayal of Julia under unbearable torture in Room 101. It highlights the Party's insidious power in eroding the most intimate bonds. Post-torture, when Winston and Julia meet, their love, once fiery and resistant, has been extinguished, replaced by a mutual indifference. This tragic transformation underscores the Party's success in obliterating personal affections.

Human Connection vs. State Control:

At its core, the theme of **Love and Sexuality** in "1984" grapples with the eternal conflict between genuine human connection and the cold, calculated control of an authoritarian state. Through Winston and Julia's relationship and their eventual fate, Orwell paints a poignant picture of the fragility of human bonds in the face of overwhelming power. The narrative serves as a stark reminder of the intrinsic human need for genuine connection, intimacy, and love and the tragedies that unfold when these are suppressed or manipulated.

Children as Instruments of the Party:

Within Orwell's grim landscape, children aren't just innocent beings; they're indoctrinated instruments of the Party. Family, an institution traditionally associated with unconditional love, is infiltrated and poisoned by the Party. Children are taught to be loyal not to their parents, but to the Party, to the point where they become spies within their own homes, reporting any hint of unorthodoxy. This treacherous dynamic erodes the foundational love and trust typically found within families, replacing it with paranoia and fear. The chilling tale of Mrs. Parsons and her children exemplifies this dystopian distortion, where her own offspring threaten to denounce her.

Emotion as Weakness and Strength:

Throughout "1984", love and emotions are portrayed as both vulnerabilities and strengths. While Winston and Julia's love offers them moments of solace and rebellion against the Party, it also becomes a point of vulnerability that the Party exploits. Their love, which once fortified their resistance, becomes the conduit for their ultimate submission. In the harrowing chambers of the Ministry of Love, it's their fear for each other's well-being that becomes a tool for their psychological torment.

The Sterility of Party Relationships:

To further understand the depth of the Party's control over love and sexuality, one must observe the relationship between Katharine and Winston. Their marriage, devoid of warmth or passion, stands as a testament to the Party's success in eradicating genuine intimacy. Katharine's view of sex as a "duty to the Party" to produce offspring starkly contrasts Julia's rebellious perspective. Such sterile relationships serve the Party's objective: eliminate personal bonds and ensure loyalty only to the state.

Orwell's exploration of love and sexuality in "1984" is not just a narrative tool but a profound commentary on the human spirit's resilience and the lengths to which totalitarian regimes can go to suppress it. Love, in all its forms, represents a deeply human experience, an innate desire to connect, understand, and belong. By manipulating and suppressing these desires, the Party aims to eliminate potential threats and maintain its stranglehold on power.

Yet, despite the bleakness of the novel's conclusion, the very existence of Winston and Julia's relationship, however fleeting, serves as a beacon of hope. It underscores the innate human yearning for genuine connection and the indomitable spirit that, even in the darkest of times, seeks out moments of love, intimacy, and understanding.

BETRAYAL THEME

In the shadowed world of "1984", betrayal isn't just a possibility; it's almost an inevitability. George Orwell paints a chilling tapestry where personal loyalties, friendships, and even deep-seated love become fragile, eventually crumbling under the oppressive weight of the Party's omnipotent gaze. This theme courses through the novel like a silent, insidious river, underscoring the moral compromises individuals make when faced with fear and coercion.

Societal Betrayal:

From the outset, citizens of Oceania have been betrayed by the very institution that purports to safeguard their interests. The Party promises prosperity, safety, and unity, but in reality, it delivers poverty, constant surveillance, and an atmosphere thick with suspicion. The very fabric of society is woven with deceit, with the Party's propaganda machines like the Ministry of Truth continuously rewriting history to fit its narrative, ensuring that the populace lives in a perpetual state of manipulated reality.

The Erosion of Personal Loyalties:

Orwell introduces us to a society where personal relationships are fraught with tension. Children, after being brainwashed by the Party, betray their parents for "thoughtcrimes", turning familial love into a potential threat. The story of the Parsons family is a grim testament to this, where Mr. Parsons, with a mix of pride and fear, narrates how his own children reported him to the Thought Police.

Winston and Julia:

The relationship between Winston and Julia is central to the exploration of betrayal in the novel. Their illicit love affair, which begins as a mutual act of rebellion, becomes fraught with paranoia as the fear of discovery looms large. Yet, in the traumatic confines of Room 101, faced with his deepest fear, Winston commits the ultimate betrayal: he chooses self-preservation over his love for Julia, pleading with O'Brien to "Do it to Julia!" It's a harrowing moment, showcasing the lengths to which individuals might go when pushed to their psychological limits.

O'Brien's Deception:

Perhaps one of the most profound acts of betrayal is O'Brien's deception. Presented initially as a potential ally, maybe even a mentor figure to Winston, O'Brien's true allegiance is a gut-wrenching revelation. He not only betrays Winston's trust but actively participates in his torture and re-education, embodying the cold, calculated cruelty of the Party.

Inner Betrayal:

Beyond external acts, "1984" delves into the personal betrayals individuals commit against themselves. Through the concept of "doublethink", the Party forces its citizens to hold two contradictory beliefs simultaneously. This constant mental gymnastics, where individuals betray their own logic and understanding, manifests the Party's control not just over actions but thoughts and beliefs.

In "1984", betrayal emerges not just as a theme but as a reflection of a broken society where trust is a luxury and survival often necessitates compromise. Orwell's exploration of betrayal — both personal and societal — is a poignant commentary on the fragility of human relationships under totalitarian regimes. It underscores the profound costs of living under an omnipotent authority, where personal loyalties are constantly tested, and the very essence of human connection becomes perilous. Through the grim landscape of betrayal in the novel, Orwell prompts readers to reflect on the value of trust, loyalty, and human integrity in the face of overwhelming adversity.

Main characters

1. Winston Smith:

Description: Winston, our protagonist, is an introspective, middle-aged man who works at the Ministry of Truth, where he alters historical records to fit the Party's ever-changing narrative.

Character Depth: Despite his seemingly mundane existence, Winston harbors deep-seated discontent with the Party and questions the reality presented to him. His rebellious thoughts, diary writings, and illicit affair with Julia are testaments to his resistance against the oppressive regime. His tragic journey, which culminates in betrayal and indoctrination, serves as the novel's bleak commentary on the individual's helplessness against totalitarian might.

2. Julia:

Description: Julia is a vibrant young woman employed in the Fiction Department of the Ministry of Truth.

Character Depth: While she outwardly adheres to Party norms, even being a member of the Anti-Sex League, Julia inwardly rebels against the Party's moral strictures. Her sexual liaisons, including her relationship with Winston, become acts of political defiance. Unlike Winston, who intellectually opposes the Party's ideology, Julia's rebellion is more personal and pragmatic, seeking pleasure and personal freedom amidst oppression.

3. O'Brien:

Description: O'Brien is an enigmatic, high-ranking Party member who initially seems to be a potential ally to Winston.

Character Depth: His articulate manner, combined with subtle hints, makes Winston believe that O'Brien might also be against the Party. However, this facade crumbles when O'Brien's true colors are revealed. He's not just loyal to the Party but is instrumental in Winston's capture, torture, and re-education. Through O'Brien, Orwell showcases the cold, calculated nature of totalitarian regimes, where humanity and empathy are subservient to power and control.

4. Big Brother:

Description: The ever-watching, omnipotent leader of the Party, Big Brother's visage is plastered everywhere, accompanied by the ominous phrase "BIG BROTHER IS WATCHING YOU."

Character Depth: What's intriguing is that Big Brother might not even be a real person but a constructed symbol of the Party's omnipresence and authority. He embodies the absolute power and surveillance state of Oceania, serving as a constant reminder of the Party's control over its citizens.

5. Mr. Charrington:

Description: An elderly man who runs a second-hand shop in the Prole district.

Character Depth: Winston and Julia rent a room above his shop for their secret meetings, believing it to be a safe haven. However, as the story unfolds, Mr. Charrington's true identity as a member of the Thought Police is revealed. His betrayal underscores the novel's theme of pervasive surveillance and the Party's far-reaching influence.

6. Syme:

Description: Syme is a co-worker of Winston's at the Ministry of Truth, involved in the creation of the Eleventh Edition of the Newspeak dictionary.

Character Depth: Intelligent and enthusiastic about his work, Syme represents the intellectual submission to the Party. Despite his loyalty, he possesses too much understanding of the Party's manipulation of language, making him a potential threat. His eventual disappearance showcases that blind obedience isn't enough; even intellectual acknowledgment of the Party's methods can lead to one's downfall.

Through these characters, Orwell paints a vivid tableau of life under a totalitarian regime, where trust is elusive, resistance is perilous, and the human spirit is constantly under siege. Each character, in their unique way, contributes to the novel's profound exploration of power, control, and the indomitable will to seek truth amidst deception.

DESCRIBE WINSTON SMITH

Winston Smith, the introspective and conflicted protagonist of George Orwell's "1984," stands as a stark representation of individuality stifled by an oppressive regime. Through his journey, Orwell weaves a tale of intellectual rebellion, personal anguish, and the crushing weight of totalitarianism.

Physical Appearance and Health:

At the very outset, *Chapter I* offers a glimpse into Winston's physicality. He's described as a man of "small but stature," with "fair hair" and a "sanguine face." As he climbs towards his flat in Victory Mansions, we're informed of the "varicose ulcer" on his right ankle, a persistent ailment that bothers him. This ulcer, aside from its literal presence, stands metaphorically as a constant reminder of the decaying society he inhabits and his own deteriorating health under the Party's rule.

Mental State and Beliefs:

Throughout the novel, Winston's introspections provide a window into a mind deeply skeptical of the Party. In *Chapter VII*, as he pens down his thoughts, he writes:

> "Freedom is the freedom to say that two plus two make four. If that is granted, all else follows."

This simple arithmetic assertion encapsulates Winston's broader defiance. To him, the Party's manipulation of truth, its capacity to declare 2 + 2 = 5, is its most pernicious crime.

Relationship with Julia:

Winston's relationship with Julia, initiated with her secret note in *Chapter VI* of *Part One*, becomes a vital avenue of his rebellion. It's not just an act of physical intimacy but a profound political statement. In *Chapter II* of *Part Two*, inside the secret rented room, their relationship blossoms, representing a sanctuary from the Party's ever-watchful eye. However, even in these moments, the shadow of the Party looms large. He observes in *Chapter IV* of *Part Two*:

> "Their embrace had been a battle, the climax a victory. It was a blow struck against the Party. It was a political act."

Encounter with O'Brien:

Winston's eventual interaction with O'Brien, whom he mistakenly believes is a fellow dissident, forms a significant aspect of his character's journey. In *Chapter II* of *Part Two*, during a clandestine meeting, O'Brien's question to Winston and Julia - "You are prepared to give your lives?" - and Winston's affirmative response underscores his deep-seated desire to overthrow the Party.

Torture and Transformation:

The harrowing chapters of Winston's imprisonment and torture in the Ministry of Love reveal the depths of his resistance and the overwhelming might of the Party. In *Chapter I* of *Part Three*, despite physical and psychological torment, Winston holds onto a sliver of resistance: his love for Julia. However, by *Chapter V*, under relentless pressure, even this final bastion crumbles. The breaking point arrives in *Chapter II* of *Part Three* with the infamous Room 101 scene, wherein Winston's deepest fears are leveraged to break his spirit. The haunting words he utters, "Do it to Julia!", signify his ultimate betrayal of his own values and love.

Conclusion:

Winston Smith, with his frailties, aspirations, and eventual capitulation, serves as a cautionary emblem of the individual's struggle against overwhelming oppression. Orwell meticulously charts Winston's trajectory, from a silent skeptic to a fervent rebel, and finally to a broken man. Through Winston, "1984" poses haunting questions about the nature of resistance, the malleability of reality, and the limits of human endurance.

DESCRIBE JULIA

Julia emerges as a figure of clandestine defiance in George Orwell's chillingly prescient novel, "1984." While on the surface she conforms to the Party's dictates, her inner world is ablaze with rebellion. Let's peel back the layers of Julia's character using specific passages and chapter references.

Physical Description and Initial Perception:

In *Chapter II*, when Winston first notices Julia at the Ministry of Truth, she is described with "thick dark hair," a "bold, aquiline face," and is athletic and graceful, "a creature that seemed to have been created to be seen in motion." Her bright red sash, emblematic of the Junior Anti-Sex League, drapes over her uniform, symbolizing her purported allegiance to Party doctrines around chastity.

Underlying Rebellion:

However, the layers of Julia's rebellion are peeled back as we proceed. In *Chapter VI*, she secretly hands Winston a note with the words "I love you" written on it, an audacious act of defiance in the watchful state. It's through this covert message that Winston and readers discern her true feelings and the undercurrent of rebellion that runs deep in her veins.

Character and Beliefs:

In *Chapter III* of *Part Two*, during their secret rendezvous in the countryside, Julia reveals her aversion to the Party's control over intimacy and relationships. Unlike Winston, Julia's rebellion is less about toppling the Party and more about finding personal, secretive ways to resist its reach. She admits:

> "They can't get inside you. If you can feel that staying human is worth while, even when it can't have any result whatever, you've beaten them."

Julia's pragmatism is further revealed when she dismisses the Party's propaganda, such as the purported wars with Eurasia or Eastasia. To her, these are mere distractions meant to keep the populace in perpetual anxiety and allegiance to the Party. Her rebellions are more tactile and immediate, such as making love or secretly consuming contraband items.

Julia's Relationship with Winston:

Their relationship, rife with danger and secrecy, flourishes in *Chapter II* of *Part Two* in a rented room above Mr. Charrington's shop, a place that seems untouched by the Party's prying eyes. Here, their bond is both a means of personal connection and an act of defiance. She tells Winston in *Chapter III* of *Part Two*:

> "You are only a rebel from the waist downwards," she told him.

This quote encapsulates her belief that rebellion against the Party is most potent when it's personal and sensual, rather than intellectual.

Conclusion:

Julia is not just a romantic interest for Winston; she embodies a different kind of resistance against the Party's tyranny. Her character serves to showcase the diverse ways in which individuals navigate and resist oppression. Through her interactions with Winston, Orwell demonstrates the complexities of rebellion, love, and trust in a society where personal freedoms are constantly under siege.

DESCRIBE O'BRIEN

O'Brien stands as one of the most enigmatic and multifaceted characters in George Orwell's "1984". He is a simultaneous embodiment of the Party's terrifying omnipotence and the illusion of rebellion. Through O'Brien's interactions with Winston, Orwell explores themes of power, manipulation, and the malleability of truth.

Introduction and Physicality:

From Winston's earliest observations in *Chapter I*, O'Brien is described as a "large, burly man with a thick neck and a coarse, humorous, brutal face." Even though he is part of the Inner Party, as his black overalls suggest, there's an intellectual depth to him that Winston senses. His face is characterized by intelligence, hinting at a formidable mind behind those "very penetrating" blue eyes.

Illusion of Rebellion:

What makes O'Brien fascinating is his dual role: both as a beacon of hope for Winston and, eventually, as the instrument of his torment. Winston, in *Chapter I*, is strangely drawn to O'Brien, thinking he might be against the Party: "One knew that it was all rubbish, so why let oneself be worried by it? In a way, the Party imposed itself most successfully on people incapable of understanding it. They could be made to accept the most flagrant violations of reality, because they never fully grasped the enormity of what was demanded of them, and were not sufficiently interested in public events to notice what was happening."

O'Brien seems to nurture this belief by dropping subtle hints, such as in *Chapter II* of *Part Two*, when he tells Winston, "We shall meet in the place where there is no darkness." This cryptic promise heightens Winston's belief that O'Brien is a fellow dissident.

Revealing True Colors:

However, as the narrative unfolds, O'Brien's true allegiance becomes terrifyingly clear. In *Chapter II* of *Part Three*, in the sterile confines of the Ministry of Love, O'Brien, as Winston's torturer, reveals his unwavering devotion to the Party. He becomes the mouthpiece of the Party's doctrine, laying bare its motives. He states:

> "Power is not a means; it is an end. One does not establish a dictatorship in order to safeguard a revolution; one makes the revolution in order to establish the dictatorship."

Manipulation of Reality:

O'Brien's psychological manipulation of Winston reaches its peak in *Chapter IV* of *Part Three*. Here, he confronts Winston's resistance to accepting the Party's control over truth. In a chilling exchange, when Winston argues about the nature of reality, O'Brien retorts:

> "Reality is not external. Reality exists in the human mind, and nowhere else."

O'Brien's intent is to break Winston, not merely physically, but mentally. He wishes to reshape Winston's perception of reality, to make him accept whatever the Party decrees as truth.

Conclusion:

O'Brien's character serves as a powerful exploration of the nature of power and the lengths to which an authoritarian regime will go to maintain it. He embodies the cold, calculating intellect of the Party — its ability to perceive dissent, to manipulate, and to break the spirit of its subjects. Through O'Brien, Orwell paints a bleak picture of a world where those in power are not bound by any moral or ethical constraints, where the very essence of truth is at the mercy of those who wield control.

DESCRIBE BIG BROTHER

Big Brother, the omnipotent and omnipresent figurehead of the Party in George Orwell's "1984," looms large over every aspect of the novel. Despite never appearing in person, Big Brother's influence is felt in every corner of the society Orwell depicts, serving as a symbol of total surveillance, unyielding power, and the profound control the Party exerts over the populace.

Physical Depiction:

From the start of the novel, we're presented with a world blanketed by Big Brother's watchful gaze. In *Chapter I*, Winston is introduced to the reader within the confines of his flat in Victory Mansions, where a "coloured poster" with an enormous face gazes down at him: "BIG BROTHER IS WATCHING YOU." The caption beneath it reads. The face is characterized by a set of "ruggedly handsome" features and piercing eyes that seem to follow one around.

Symbol of Totalitarian Control:

Big Brother is more than just a leader; he is a symbol. The very idea of Big Brother represents the Party's omniscience. Everywhere, from coins to posters, his image is a constant reminder of the Party's watchful eyes. Winston observes in *Chapter I* of *Part One* that one cannot escape the gaze of Big Brother. The omnipresent telescreens broadcast his image and relay his messages.

Embodiment of the Party:

Big Brother serves as the embodiment of the Party's ideals and objectives.

s ideals and objectives. The proclamations and slogans of the Party are often associated with his visage. *Chapter III* outlines the disorienting reality of the Two Minutes Hate, a daily ritual wherein Party members express their collective loathing for enemies of the state. In this ritual, Big Brother's image brings a sense of calm, showcasing him as the savior and protector against external and internal threats.

Immutable and Unchanging:

One of the more eerie aspects of Big Brother's presence is his seeming immortality and timelessness. In *Chapter III*, the Party slogan asserts, "Big Brother is infallible and all-powerful." There's no past or present leader; there's only Big Brother, an eternal figure that has always been and will always be. This permanence further enforces the idea of the Party's never-ending reign.

Ambiguity of Existence:

Despite Big Brother's pervasive presence, Orwell intentionally leaves it ambiguous as to whether he is a real individual or just a fabricated symbol. O'Brien, when questioned by Winston in *Chapter III* of *Part Three* about Big Brother's existence, responds ambiguously: "Big Brother exists... Big Brother will never die." The implication is that whether or not Big Brother is a tangible person is irrelevant; his purpose as a symbol of power and control is what truly matters.

Conclusion:

Through Big Brother, Orwell crafts a potent symbol of the dangers of unchecked power and the lengths to which totalitarian regimes will go to maintain control. The omnipresent gaze of Big Brother serves as a chilling reminder of the loss of privacy and freedom in a world where the state wields absolute authority. It's a world where reality is manufactured, truths are mutable, and the individual is always subordinate to the will of the Party. Big Brother epitomizes this dystopian vision, a figure that encapsulates the horrors of absolute power in the hands of the few.

DESCRIBE MR. CHARRINGTON

Mr. Charrington, a seemingly benign elderly shopkeeper in Orwell's "1984," emerges as a surprisingly pivotal character, deeply intertwined with the novel's overarching themes of surveillance, betrayal, and the insidious reach of the Party.

Physical Appearance and Initial Impression:

Mr. Charrington is introduced in *Chapter VIII* of *Part One* when Winston enters his second-hand shop in the Prole district. He's depicted as a frail old man with "thick spectacles" and a "mild and benevolent appearance." His slow movements, thin silver hair, and a "long nose which was like a beak" give him an air of gentle antiquity, reminiscent of a bygone era.

Keeper of the Past:

Mr. Charrington's shop brims with items from the past, which the Party has endeavored to erase or rewrite. It is here that Winston buys the diary where he first begins to express his rebellious thoughts. Mr. Charrington appears to appreciate the beauty and stories of older things, sharing Winston's nostalgia for the past. He recites a fragment of a rhyme about churches in *Chapter VIII* of *Part One*, which intrigues Winston and leads to further interactions between the two.

The Room Above the Shop:

The relationship between Winston and Mr. Charrington deepens when the shopkeeper shows him a room above his shop in *Chapter II* of *Part Two*. This room, free from the prying eyes of the telescreen, becomes a sanctuary for Winston and Julia, allowing their illicit relationship to blossom. Its antiquated charm, embodied by an "old-fashioned glass clock with a twelve-hour face" and an engraving of a church, underscores the themes of memory and the passage of time.

A Shocking Betrayal:

However, Orwell masterfully shatters the reader's and Winston's perceptions in *Chapter VIII* of *Part Three*. In a sudden and shocking twist, during Winston and Julia's arrest, it's revealed that Mr. Charrington is not what he seems. His antiquated appearance is a disguise; he's actually a member of the Thought Police. The frailty vanishes, replaced by "a different face, the face of a man of about thirty-five, with a heavy black moustache and ruggedly handsome features." This revelation is a brutal testament to the Party's omnipresence and the extent to which it will go to root out and extinguish dissent.

Symbolic Significance:

Mr. Charrington's dual identity — both as a seemingly benign old shop-keeper and as a cunning agent of the Party — serves as a stark embodiment of the novel's themes of duplicity, surveillance, and the treacherous nature of trust in a totalitarian society. His character underlines the idea that rebellion, or even the mere thought of it, is nearly impossible when the system you're rebelling against is always two steps ahead.

Conclusion:

In the figure of Mr. Charrington, Orwell offers a chilling portrayal of betrayal and the omnipotent reach of the Party. Just as Winston seeks solace in the past, believing it to be unalterable and genuine, Mr. Charrington's shop and the room above it lure him with a false sense of security, only to ultimately betray him. This subterfuge reinforces the novel's dark message about the insidiousness of totalitarian control and the dangers of misplaced trust.

DESCRIBE SYME

Syme, though not a central character in George Orwell's "1984", plays a significant role in elucidating the Party's manipulation of language and its impact on thought. His existence, and subsequent erasure, reflect the Party's ruthless approach to any potential threats, no matter how loyal or enthusiastic the individual may be.

Physical Appearance and Demeanor:

Syme is introduced in *Chapter V* of *Part One* as a "tiny creature" with a "shrunken face" and "large, protuberant eyes" that give him a scholarly, yet somewhat eerie, appearance. His movements, characterized by a certain precision, mirror his intellectual acumen.

Profession and Newspeak:

Syme is a philologist specializing in the development of the Eleventh Edition of the Newspeak dictionary. He has an almost fanatical enthusiasm for his work. In his conversations with Winston in *Chapter V* of *Part One*, Syme elucidates the principles behind Newspeak. The Party's intention is to reduce the number of words and thereby limit the range of thought. Syme speaks passionately about destroying words: "Don't you see that the whole aim of Newspeak is to narrow the range of thought? [...] Every year fewer and fewer words, and the range of consciousness always a little smaller." His pride in this endeavor underscores his loyalty to the Party and his unyielding belief in its mission.

Intellectual Awareness:

Though a staunch supporter of the Party's cause, Syme possesses a keen intellectual awareness that proves to be his downfall. He understands the Party's motives with a clarity that most other members lack. His insights into the purpose of Newspeak give the reader a clearer understanding of the Party's goals. In *Chapter V* of *Part One*, Syme remarks, "By 2050—earlier, probably—all real knowledge of Oldspeak will have disappeared. The whole literature of the past will have been destroyed." This acknowledgment of the Party's manipulation of history and culture is profound.

Winston's Prediction and Syme's Disappearance:

Winston, with his discerning understanding of the Party's machinations, predicts early on that Syme's intelligence and understanding will lead to his vaporization. In *Chapter V* of *Part One*, Winston notes, "One of these days, thought Winston with sudden deep conviction, Syme will be vaporized. He is too intelligent. He sees too clearly and speaks too plainly." Winston's premonition comes true by *Chapter VII* of *Part Two*, when Syme, despite his unwavering dedication, disappears without a trace, erased from the Party's records and from the memories of his peers.

Symbolic Significance:

Syme serves as a cautionary example of the consequences of possessing too much awareness in a society that values blind loyalty above all else. His erasure, despite his loyalty and contributions, demonstrates the Party's fear of intellectualism. Anyone who understands the Party's true intent, even if they support it, is a threat.

Conclusion:

Syme's character serves as a chilling testament to the Party's total control and its capacity to erase individuals who might pose even the slightest risk. His erasure from existence, despite his dedication and understanding, highlights the peril of intellectual insight in Orwell's dystopian world. Through Syme, the novel underscores the deeply unsettling idea that understanding can be just as dangerous as dissent.

Minor characters

1. Ampleforth:

Description: A poet working in the Records Department at the Ministry of Truth, Ampleforth's job is to modify classic literature to align with Party ideology.

Role: His arrest for leaving the word "God" in a Kipling poem underscores the Party's intolerance of even the slightest oversight, no matter the loyalty or intentions of the individual.

2. Tom Parsons:

Description: Parsons is Winston's naive and loyal co-worker and neighbor. He's an ardent supporter of the Party and involves himself enthusiastically in community activities.

Role: Despite his loyalty, he's turned in for thoughtcrime by his own children. His character portrays the dangers of blind obedience and the horrifying reality of children betraying their parents in the Party's name.

3. Mrs. Parsons:

Description: The weary wife of Tom Parsons, she's overwhelmed by her children's aggressive indoctrination.

Role: Mrs. Parsons embodies the struggles of domestic life in Oceania, where even home isn't a sanctuary but a place fraught with tension and fear.

4. The Parsons Children:

Description: The zealous offspring of Tom and Mrs. Parsons.

Role: They exemplify the Party's effective brainwashing from a young age. They spy on adults, including their parents, and are fervent members of the Spies, a youth organization that promotes Party loyalty.

5. Katharine:

Description: Winston's estranged wife, often referred to as "the human soundtrack."

Role: Her rigid adherence to the Party's stance on sex — that it's a duty to the Party for procreation — contrasts with Julia's more rebellious view on sexuality. Katharine represents the emotional void created by the Party's interference in personal relationships.

6. Jones, Aaronson, and Rutherford:

Description: Former Party leaders who were arrested, tortured into confessing to crimes they didn't commit, and then executed.

Role: They signify the Party's ability and willingness to rewrite history. Winston sees a photograph that proves their innocence, reinforcing the idea that the Party constructs its own truth.

7. The Proles:

Description: Representing 85% of Oceania's population, they're the working-class citizens outside of Party membership.

Role: Though Winston believes that "if there is hope, it lies in the proles," the novel depicts them as largely apathetic to the Party's machinations, concerned more with their daily lives. They serve as a representation of a subdued majority, showing that without consciousness or resistance, change is impossible.

8. The Old Man in the Pub:

Description: An elderly prole Winston attempts to engage in conversation about life before the Party's reign.

Role: His inability to give Winston clear answers about the past underscores the loss of collective memory and history in Oceania.

9. The Red-Armed Prole Woman:

Description: A robust prole woman whom Winston observes from his rented room above Mr. Charrington's shop.

Role: Her enduring spirit and song symbolize the unbreakable human spirit. Julia and Winston view her as a symbol of hope and resilience.

10. Goldstein:

Description: The alleged leader of the Brotherhood and author of "The Book." He's the Party's designated enemy, used to incite hatred and loyalty among citizens.

Role: Though his actual existence is questionable, Goldstein's image serves as a tool for the Party to channel citizens' negative emotions and solidify their power.

These minor characters, though not as central as Winston or Julia, play crucial roles in fleshing out the world of "1984." They add layers to the narrative, illustrating the omnipresence of the Party's influence and the varied ways individuals react to and are shaped by oppression. Through them, Orwell paints a multifaceted picture of a society where every corner, every individual, is touched by the chilling hand of totalitarianism.

DESCRIBE THE CHARACTER'S CLOTHING

In George Orwell's "1984", clothing plays a role in depicting the drab, uniform, and repressive nature of the society under the Party's control. Here's a description of the attire based on the text:

1. **Party Members:**

   - **Outer Party:** Winston and other members of the Outer Party wear a uniform of blue overalls. These are described as being of a coarser make.

   - **Inner Party:** Members of the Inner Party, like O'Brien, wear black overalls, which distinguishes them from the Outer Party and denotes their higher rank.

2. **Proles (Proletarians):**

   - The Proles, who are not members of the Party and represent the majority of the population, don't have a specific uniform like the Party members. Their clothing is described as being more varied and colorful, representing their relatively unrestricted (though still impoverished) lives. The woman singing outside Mr. Charrington's shop, whom Winston observes, is described wearing a "rose-colored" dress.

1. **The Thought Police:**

   ○ They are not described in detail in terms of attire, but they often blend in with the rest of the population to spy and capture thought criminals. However, when they conduct raids or arrests, they might be identified by their black uniforms.

2. **Physical Jerks:**

   ○ In the morning, Winston is mentioned participating in the Physical Jerks, a mandatory exercise routine. For this, he wears the blue overalls, the same attire he wears daily.

3. **Anti-Sex League:**

   ○ Julia, when Winston first becomes aware of her, wears a red sash around her waist, signifying her membership in the Junior Anti-Sex League. This sash is emblematic of chastity and is worn by those who promote celibacy, except for procreation purposes sanctioned by the Party.

The clothing in "1984" is emblematic of the society's values: uniformity, conformity, and control. Personal expression or individualism is minimized, and even the differences in clothing (like the color differences between Inner and Outer Party uniforms) serve to delineate rank and maintain hierarchies.

IMPORTANT RELATIONSHIPS

the relationships in George Orwell's "1984" are crucial in delineating the social fabric of a totalitarian society, illustrating how the Party's manipulation affects interpersonal dynamics. Here's a detailed look at the prominent relationships in the novel:

1. **Winston and Julia:**
   - **Nature of Relationship:** They share a passionate, rebellious love affair, and through their liaison, they defy the Party's prohibition against individualism, personal attachment, and sexual pleasure.

   - **Reference:** Their clandestine meetings begin in *Chapter II of Part Two* when Julia slips Winston a note confessing her love. Their relationship grows in the rented room above Mr. Charrington's shop, where they believe they're safe from the Party's prying eyes.

   - **Significance:** This relationship symbolizes a rebellion against the Party's ethos. While they can't overthrow the Party, their love is a personal revolt. It's ephemeral but offers a brief respite from the omnipresent oppression.

2. **Winston and O'Brien:**
   - **Nature of Relationship:** Winston mistakenly believes O'Brien is an ally, a fellow dissident against the Party's regime. However, O'Brien later reveals himself as a devout Party loyalist, tasked with torturing and "reintegrating" dissenters like Winston.

- **Reference:** Winston's initial hope is seen when he dreams of O'Brien saying, "We shall meet in the place where there is no darkness," in *Chapter VII of Part One*. This is juxtaposed against the reality in *Part Three* when O'Brien becomes Winston's torturer in the Ministry of Love.

- **Significance:** O'Brien's betrayal underscores the futility of rebellion in a society where trust is a liability. Their dynamic reflects the hopelessness of personal connections and the omnipresence of betrayal.

3. Winston and Big Brother:

- **Nature of Relationship:** While they never meet (and it's unclear if Big Brother is a real person or merely a symbol), Winston feels a potent mix of fear, hatred, and fascination towards him. Big Brother's omnipresent gaze embodies the Party's absolute control.

- **Reference:** The phrase "BIG BROTHER IS WATCHING YOU" is omnipresent throughout the novel, a clear reminder of the Party's surveillance and Winston's relationship with this entity.

- **Significance:** This relationship represents the individual's powerlessness against the might of a totalitarian regime. By the end, Winston's love for Big Brother, induced by torture and brainwashing, signifies his complete subjugation.

4. Winston and Parsons:

- **Nature of Relationship:** Parsons is Winston's naive and loyal neighbor. Their interactions highlight the contrast between blind loyalty and rebellious cognizance.

- **Reference:** In *Chapter I of Part Three*, inside the Ministry of

Love, Winston encounters Parsons, who's been reported by his daughter for thoughtcrime. His unwavering faith in the Party, even when betrayed by his kin, is evident.

- **Significance:** Through Parsons, Orwell paints a bleak picture of a society where familial bonds are secondary to loyalty to the Party.

5. Julia and O'Brien:

- **Nature of Relationship:** Much like Winston, Julia is duped into trusting O'Brien. Together, they visit him, erroneously believing they're joining a rebellion against the Party.

- **Reference:** Their trust is betrayed when, in *Chapter VIII of Part Two*, during their meeting at O'Brien's apartment, it's revealed much later that they're being set up.

- **Significance:** This relationship emphasizes the depth of the Party's deception and how it ensnares even those most wary of its tricks.

Not to forget the notable yet less crucial relationships, let's look at the following;

1. Winston and Mr. Charrington:

- **Nature of Relationship:** Initially, Mr. Charrington appears as a kind old shopkeeper who rents Winston and Julia the room above his shop for their secret meetings. He represents a connection to the past. However, he is later revealed as a member of the Thought Police.

- **Reference:** In *Chapter VIII of Part Two*, Winston feels a sense of trust and nostalgia while interacting with Mr. Charrington. But this is shattered in *Chapter X of Part Two*, during the raid on the secret room, when Mr. Charrington's true identity comes to the fore.

- **Significance:** This twist serves as a devastating reminder of the Party's extensive surveillance apparatus. It emphasizes that in the world of "1984", trust is a luxury that can lead to one's downfall.

2. Julia and Katharine (Winston's wife):

- **Nature of Relationship:** Though Katharine and Julia never meet, the contrast between them in Winston's mind is sharp. Katharine was Winston's wife, and their relationship was cold and joyless, characterized by the Party's dictums on marital duties and procreation. In contrast, Julia represents passion, rebellion, and individualism.

- **Reference:** In *Chapter VI of Part One*, Winston recalls his estranged relationship with Katharine, describing their sexual encounters as a "duty to the Party". This is a stark contrast to his liaison with Julia.

- **Significance:** Through these relationships, Orwell critiques the Party's attempts to strip away human emotion and intimacy, turning even the most personal acts into political ones.

3. Parsons and His Children:

- **Nature of Relationship:** Parsons is blindly loyal to the Party, and he's proud of his children being part of the Party's youth organization, the Spies. However, it's his daughter who reports him for committing thoughtcrime.

- **Reference:** In *Chapter I of Part Three*, Parsons reveals with a strange kind of pride that his daughter was the one who turned him in, showing how deeply the Party's indoctrination runs.

- **Significance:** This relationship underscores the Party's success in eroding family loyalties and replacing them with loyalty to the Party alone. The children's role as informants for the Party instills a sense of paranoia, even within family units.

4. Syme and Winston:

- **Nature of Relationship:** Syme, a colleague of Winston's at the Ministry of Truth, is an intelligent philologist working on the Eleventh Edition of the Newspeak dictionary. Though they aren't close friends, their interactions provide a profound insight into the Party's manipulation of language.

- **Reference:** In *Chapter V of Part One*, during their conversation in the canteen, Syme delves into the intricacies of Newspeak and its intended purpose – to narrow the range of thought.

- **Significance:** Syme's dedication to the Party's mission and his eventual disappearance highlight the dangers of being "too intelligent" or perceptive in a society that demands unquestioning obedience.

Conclusion:

Each of these relationships offers a unique lens through which to view the dystopian world of "1984". They emphasize the erosion of trust, the fragility of human connections, and the depth of the Party's control over individuals. Through these intricately woven interpersonal dynamics, Orwell illustrates the devastating consequences of a society that sacrifices its humanity at the altar of absolute power.

WINSTON AND JULIA

Winston and Julia's relationship is one of the central elements in George Orwell's "1984." This relationship stands as a symbol of rebellion against the Party's repressive regime, but it's also a deep exploration of human intimacy, trust, and betrayal under the shadow of totalitarianism.

1. The Beginning of Their Relationship:

- **Nature:** Their relationship begins with a note from Julia to Winston that reads, "I love you."

- **Reference:** In *Chapter X of Part One*, Winston is both surprised and intrigued when he receives this message.

- **Significance:** This note sets the stage for their secret meetings and becomes the initial step in their combined resistance against the Party's stringent control over personal relationships.

2. Secret Meetings:

- **Nature:** Winston and Julia start meeting in secret, often in remote locations away from surveillance.

- **Reference:** In *Chapter II of Part Two*, they have their first intimate encounter in a secluded meadow, away from the prying eyes of the Party.

- **Significance:** These secret trysts are acts of rebellion against the Party, which has criminalized such intimate relations outside of approved marriages.

3. The Room Above Mr. Charrington's Shop:

- **Nature:** The rented room becomes their sanctuary, a place seemingly untouched by the Party's influence, adorned with remnants of the past.

- **Reference:** Described in multiple chapters, including *Chapter IV of Part Two*, the room is where they believe they are free from the watchful eyes of the Party.

- **Significance:** This space symbolizes a fleeting bubble of personal freedom and privacy in a society where both are virtually non-existent.

4. Political Views:

- **Nature:** Winston is ideologically opposed to the Party, driven by a sense of moral outrage. Julia, on the other hand, is more pragmatic; she rebels by breaking the Party's rules without deeply analyzing or confronting the Party's ideology.

- **Reference:** In *Chapter III of Part Two*, during one of their conversations in the rented room, Julia expresses her disdain for the Party, but it's clear her understanding of rebellion is more personal than political.

- **Significance:** Their contrasting views highlight the different paths of resistance within the society. Winston's is intellectual and deeply philosophical, while Julia's is immediate and tangible.

5. Betrayal:

- **Nature:** After their capture, under the intense torture and psychological manipulation in the Ministry of Love, both Winston and Julia betray each other.

- **Reference:** In *Chapter II of Part Three*, O'Brien successfully manipulates Winston into betraying Julia using his worst fear: rats.

- **Significance:** Their betrayals highlight the terrifying effectiveness of the Party's tactics. The Party doesn't just want obedience; they want to invade the deepest sanctums of human emotion and loyalty, proving that in the end, under enough pressure, everyone breaks.

6. Post-Betrayal:

- **Nature:** After their respective releases, Winston and Julia meet again but find that their feelings for each other have changed. The passionate bond is broken, replaced by a sense of loss and resignation.

- **Reference:** In *Chapter VI of Part Three*, during their brief meeting in the park, it's evident that the emotional core of their relationship has been irrevocably damaged.

- **Significance:** The Party's victory over their relationship underscores its ultimate goal: to control not just actions but thoughts, feelings, and loyalties.

Conclusion:

Winston and Julia's relationship in "1984" serves multiple purposes. It's a beacon of hope, representing personal rebellion against a faceless, omnipotent regime. Yet, it's also a tragic reminder of the fragility of human connections under the relentless weight of totalitarian control. Through their love and eventual betrayal, Orwell paints a bleak portrait of the human spirit's vulnerability when faced with insurmountable oppression.

WINSTON AND O'BRIEN

The relationship between Winston and O'Brien is a deeply intricate and psychologically charged element of "1984." While Winston's relationship with Julia embodies passion and rebellion, his dynamic with O'Brien delves into the realm of intellect, manipulation, and the nature of power under totalitarianism.

1. Initial Perception:

- **Nature:** Winston initially sees O'Brien as a potential ally against the Party. He believes that O'Brien shares his anti-Party sentiments.

- **Reference:** In *Chapter I of Part One*, Winston notes a certain look in O'Brien's eyes, which he interprets as a sign of shared dissent against the Party.

- **Significance:** This belief showcases Winston's desperation for comradeship in his silent rebellion. It also establishes the foundation for O'Brien's subsequent manipulation.

2. The Brief Meeting:

- **Nature:** In a brief encounter, O'Brien makes a cryptic comment about the "10th edition" of the Newspeak dictionary, which further cements Winston's belief that O'Brien is part of the resistance.

- **Reference:** In *Chapter VIII of Part One*, O'Brien's words create a sense of mutual understanding and conspiracy between them.

- **Significance:** This event plants the seed for Winston's eventual downfall, as his trust in O'Brien makes him more vulnerable to the Party's trap.

3. The "Brotherhood":
- **Nature:** O'Brien eventually invites Winston and Julia to his luxurious apartment, where he seemingly inducts them into the Brotherhood, an alleged resistance group against the Party.

- **Reference:** In *Chapter VIII of Part Two*, O'Brien goes through the motions of initiating them, even providing them with a subversive book supposedly written by the Brotherhood's leader, Goldstein.

- **Significance:** The charade serves as bait, making Winston and Julia more bold and reckless in their actions and beliefs, effectively setting the stage for their capture.

4. Torture and Indoctrination:
- **Nature:** After Winston's arrest, he discovers that O'Brien is not a rebel but a loyal Party member. O'Brien becomes Winston's interrogator and torturer in the Ministry of Love.

- **Reference:** Throughout *Part Three*, particularly from *Chapter II onwards*, O'Brien engages in psychological and physical torture to "cure" Winston of his rebellious thoughts.

- **Significance:** The switch from potential ally to torturer signifies the Party's all-encompassing deceit and power. O'Brien's methods go beyond mere physical pain; he seeks to intrude into Winston's mind, to reshape his very perception of reality.

5. Doublethink and Reality Manipulation:

- **Nature:** O'Brien's interactions with Winston during the torture sessions are marked by discussions about the nature of reality, truth, and power. He forces Winston to accept the Party's version of reality, even if it's contradictory.

- **Reference:** In *Chapter III of Part Three*, O'Brien famously says, "Oceania has always been at war with Eastasia," a direct contradiction to the actual facts but something he forces Winston to believe.

- **Significance:** These sessions are not just about breaking Winston but also demonstrating the Party's ultimate control over truth and reality. O'Brien becomes the mouthpiece of the Party's philosophy, emphasizing that power is the ultimate goal and that reality is what the Party deems it to be.

6. The Ultimate Betrayal:

- **Nature:** O'Brien's manipulation culminates in Winston's ultimate betrayal – of his own beliefs and of Julia.

- **Reference:** In *Chapter IV of Part Three*, using Winston's fear of rats, O'Brien pushes him to the point where he screams, "Do it to Julia!", forsaking his love to save himself.

- **Significance:** O'Brien's systematic breaking of Winston's spirit demonstrates the extent to which the Party will go to ensure total loyalty and the eradication of independent thought.

Conclusion:

Winston and O'Brien's relationship is a dark journey into the heart of totalitarian control. Through their interactions, Orwell explores the malleability of reality under oppressive regimes, the fragility of individual belief when faced with overwhelming force, and the lengths to which a regime will go to maintain power. O'Brien's betrayal and manipulation of Winston underscore the novel's central themes of power, control, and the subjective nature of truth.

WINSTON AND BIG BROTHER

Winston Smith's relationship with Big Brother is one of profound psychological complexity. It encapsulates the essence of life under a totalitarian regime. Big Brother, as a figure, represents omnipotence, omnipresence, and the omniscient gaze of the Party. Winston's dynamic with Big Brother charts his internal struggles, from silent rebellion to eventual submission.

1. Big Brother as the Omnipresent Overlord:

- **Nature:** Big Brother is the face of the Party. His visage is seen on posters, coins, and telescreens, constantly reminding citizens of his watchful gaze with the warning: "BIG BROTHER IS WATCHING YOU."

- **Reference:** In *Chapter I of Part One*, Winston is introduced to the reader within the confines of his apartment, where the "BIG BROTHER IS WATCHING YOU" poster is conspicuously displayed.

- **Significance:** This immediate introduction sets the tone for the omnipresence of Big Brother throughout the novel. It establishes an environment of constant surveillance and intimidation.

2. Winston's Silent Rebellion:

- **Nature:** Initially, Winston harbors a deep-seated resentment against Big Brother. He feels suffocated by the Party's control and Big Brother's constant surveillance.

- **Reference:** Winston's diary entries, especially his act of writing "DOWN WITH BIG BROTHER" repeatedly in *Chapter I of Part One*, are direct acts of rebellion against the figure.

- **Significance:** These acts demonstrate Winston's initial resistance to the Party's brainwashing, though he is well aware of the dire consequences should his dissent be discovered.

3. Fear and Paranoia:

- **Nature:** The fear of Big Brother is deeply ingrained in Winston and other Party members. This fear keeps them in check and ensures their loyalty.

- **Reference:** In *Chapter II of Part One*, Winston is jolted into paranoia when he believes the voice from the telescreen is addressing him directly, showcasing the extent of Big Brother's intrusive reach.

- **Significance:** The telescreens, as extensions of Big Brother, become tools of psychological torment, ensuring conformity and quashing rebellion.

4. Winston's Hope of Overthrow:

- **Nature:** Winston fantasizes about a revolution against the Party and the downfall of Big Brother.

- **Reference:** In his diary, in *Chapter VII of Part One*, Winston writes about the proles, believing that if there is hope, it lies with them, hoping they might one day rise against the oppressive regime of Big Brother.

- **Significance:** Despite the overwhelming control of Big Brother, Winston clings to a fragile hope of overthrowing this omnipotent figure.

5. Final Submission and Adoration:

- **Nature:** After enduring intense psychological and physical torture at the hands of the Party, Winston's resistance is shattered. His feelings towards Big Brother transform from resentment to acceptance and even love.

- **Reference:** In the final chapter, *Chapter VI of Part Three*, after a long journey of rebellion and re-education, Winston's transformation is complete when he tearfully realizes he loves Big Brother.

- **Significance:** Orwell portrays the ultimate triumph of the Party—breaking the individual's spirit to the point where they not only obey but also love their oppressor.

Conclusion:

Winston's relationship with Big Brother evolves from one of quiet resistance to overt adulation, encapsulating the novel's overarching themes of power, control, and the malleability of human perception and emotion under extreme duress. Big Brother, as both a symbolic and omnipresent figure, serves as a constant reminder of the Party's inescapable dominance in the lives of its subjects. Through Winston's interactions with this pervasive entity, Orwell paints a grim picture of life under totalitarian rule and the lengths to which such a regime will go to maintain its grip on power.

WINSTON AND PARSONS

Winston Smith and Tom Parsons share a relationship that is emblematic of the society in which they live. As neighbors and coworkers at the Ministry of Truth, their interactions provide insight into the everyday realities of life in Airstrip One under the Party's control. Their relationship also illustrates the contrast between a skeptic of the Party (Winston) and a devout follower (Parsons).

1. Description of Parsons:

- **Nature:** Parsons is depicted as a fervent follower of the Party, embodying blind loyalty and obliviousness.

- **Reference:** Early in the novel, in *Chapter II*, Winston describes Parsons as a "fat, sweaty," and "obnoxious" man, highlighting his physical unattractiveness and perhaps indirectly suggesting the ugliness of blind conformity. His constant sweatiness can be seen as a symbol of his feverish, uncritical devotion to the Party.

2. Parsons's Children:

- **Nature:** Parsons is proud of his children, who are zealous members of the Junior Spies, but they also symbolize the dangerous extent of Party indoctrination.

- **Reference:** In *Chapter II*, Parsons speaks with pride about his children setting up a trap to catch Eurasian spies. However, the dangers of such brainwashing become evident when, later in the novel, in *Part Two, Chapter X*, his own daughter denounces him as a thoughtcriminal. Winston finds a twisted irony in this; the child's indoctrination is so complete that she'll betray her own father for the Party's cause.

3. Parsons's Beliefs vs. Winston's Skepticism:

- **Nature:** Throughout the novel, the juxtaposition between Parsons's blind loyalty and Winston's increasing skepticism is evident.

- **Reference:** In *Chapter II*, Parsons is entirely uncritical of the Party's practices, such as the Two Minutes Hate, which he participates in with gusto. Winston, on the other hand, is deeply disturbed by these spectacles.

4. Parsons in the Ministry of Truth:

- **Nature:** Parsons's job at the Ministry of Truth highlights the mundanity and pointlessness of many Party tasks.

- **Reference:** Winston notes in *Chapter IV* that Parsons's job involves working on a "sub-committee of a sub-committee," which deals with minor technicalities in the production of propaganda. This contrasts with Winston's more directly manipulative role in altering historical records.

5. The Ultimate Betrayal:

- **Nature:** The Party's ability to turn its most loyal followers into enemies is showcased in Parsons's downfall.

- **Reference:** In *Part Three, Chapter I*, Winston encounters Parsons in the Ministry of Love. Parsons has been reported by his own daughter for muttering "Down with Big Brother" in his sleep. Instead of feeling wronged, he expresses gratitude that his child has saved him from himself, highlighting his undying devotion to the Party. Winston is both horrified and saddened by this display of brainwashing.

Conclusion:

The relationship between Winston and Parsons serves as a lens through which Orwell examines the effects of totalitarianism on both the skeptics and the believers. Parsons, despite his unquestioning loyalty, falls victim to the Party's capricious cruelty, underscoring the novel's message about the dangers of unchecked power and the fragility of individual rights and freedoms.

Julia and O'Brien

Julia and O'Brien's relationship is enigmatic and primarily indirect, seen through the lens of Winston's perceptions and interactions with both characters. While both Julia and O'Brien are pivotal in Winston's life, their direct interactions in the narrative are limited. Nevertheless, the brief crossroads of their paths provide crucial moments in the plot.

1. **Julia's Initial Perception of O'Brien:**
   - **Nature:** Julia, like Winston, suspects that O'Brien might be a covert dissident or an ally against the Party.

   - **Reference:** In *Chapter II of Part Two*, during one of Winston and Julia's secret meetings, they discuss O'Brien. Julia expresses the belief that O'Brien might be against the Party when she states, "I'm sure he's against them [The Party]."

   - **Significance:** This shared belief binds Winston and Julia further, nurturing their hopes of a potential rebellion.

2. **The Invitation to O'Brien's Apartment:**
   - **Nature:** O'Brien's invitation to both Winston and Julia seems like a gesture of trust and alliance, intensifying their belief in his dissent.

   - **Reference:** In *Chapter VII of Part Two*, O'Brien invites Winston and Julia to his apartment, where they are momentarily free from the prying eyes of the Party and the omnipresent telescreens. Here,

O'Brien discusses the Brotherhood and even provides them with Goldstein's forbidden book.

- **Significance:** This meeting cements Winston and Julia's trust in O'Brien. It's a turning point, as they believe they've found a powerful ally within the Party's ranks.

3. Betrayal and Realization:
- **Nature:** The belief that O'Brien is a fellow dissident is shattered when it's revealed he has played an elaborate ruse to trap both Winston and Julia.

- **Reference:** In *Chapter III of Part Three*, during their imprisonment, Winston and Julia come to understand O'Brien's true role. O'Brien admits his involvement in their capture, telling Winston, "They got me a long time ago," when Winston shouts, "They've got you too!" This moment signifies O'Brien's long-standing loyalty to the Party.

- **Significance:** The realization of O'Brien's betrayal is pivotal. It showcases the Party's extensive reach and its capacity to manipulate its citizens' beliefs and perceptions.

4. Julia's Resistance and Breakdown:
- **Nature:** While Julia's interactions with O'Brien directly are minimal, it's inferred that she undergoes her form of "re-education" and torture under the Party's directives.

- **Reference:** In *Chapter VI of Part Three*, during a secret and brief reunion after their respective releases, Julia reveals to Winston the extent of her torture, saying, "They threatened to hurt you if I didn't give you up." This suggests her exposure to similar torments that Winston faced at the hands of O'Brien.

- **Significance:** This serves as a testament to the Party's ruthless and unyielding approach to quashing dissent, using any means necessary, including exploiting personal relationships.

Conclusion:

Julia and O'Brien's direct relationship is not extensively explored in the novel, but the intersections of their paths, largely influenced by their relationships with Winston, form a pivotal foundation in the narrative. Through them, Orwell delineates the themes of betrayal, manipulation, hope, and the shattering of illusions in the face of totalitarian power.

CONFLICTS

"1984" is rife with various conflicts, both external and internal, which serve to illuminate the novel's dark themes and messages. These conflicts help shape the narrative, the characters' development, and the depiction of the dystopian world of Oceania. Let's delve into these conflicts, referencing specific elements of the text:

1. Individual vs. State (Man vs. Society):

- **Detailed Description:** The totalitarian regime seeks to obliterate individuality, aiming to turn each citizen into a mere extension of the Party's will. Winston's attempts to assert his individuality and independent thought represent an existential threat to the Party's dominance. His struggles encapsulate the battle between the desire for personal freedom and the crushing weight of state control.

- **Reference:** Throughout the novel, we see the suppression of individuality, from the Party's banning of personal relationships not sanctioned by the state to the Thought Police's eradication of unorthodox thoughts. Winston's secret diary acts as an assertion of his own voice against the homogenizing force of the Party.

2. Internal Conflict (Man vs. Self):

- **Detailed Description:** Winston's journey is fraught with self-doubt. While part of him rebels against the Party, another part fears the consequences of such rebellion. His internal conflict is exacerbated by the Party's manipulation of reality, which makes him question his own sanity.

- **Reference:** When Winston writes in his diary, he often questions the veracity of his own memories, asking at one point: "Was it a fact, or was it a delusion?"

3. Conflict of Truth vs. Reality (Man vs. Reality):

- **Detailed Description:** The Party's manipulation of the past and control over information creates a world where objective truth is constantly shifting. This conflict touches on the philosophical question of what constitutes reality. For the Party, reality is what it dictates.

- **Reference:** The work of the Ministry of Truth, where Winston is employed, revolves around altering historical records to fit the Party's current narrative. As O'Brien tells Winston during his torture, "Whatever the Party holds to be the truth is the truth."

4. Physical Conflict (Man vs. Man):

- **Detailed Description:** The Party does not only wage a psychological war against its citizens but also employs physical means to subdue and control them. Torture, public hangings, and war are visceral manifestations of this conflict.

- **Reference:** Winston's eventual arrest and the brutal torture he undergoes in the Ministry of Love represent this physical conflict. Scenes like the forced viewing of executions amplify the visceral nature of the Party's control.

5. Conflict of Love and Loyalty vs. Oppression:

- **Detailed Description:** Personal relationships threaten the Party's absolute control over its citizens. The love between Winston and Julia becomes a form of rebellion, as it represents a loyalty and passion directed somewhere other than Big Brother.

- **Reference:** The Party's attempt to eradicate personal loyalties is evident when children are encouraged to betray their parents for unorthodox thoughts. Winston and Julia's secret meetings and the sharing of forbidden pleasures, such as real chocolate, underscore their defiance.

6. Intellectual Conflict:
- **Detailed Description:** The novel delves into deep philosophical discussions, especially during Winston's interactions with O'Brien. These debates touch upon the nature of power, reality, and the mechanisms of control.

- **Reference:** One of the most chilling moments in the novel is when O'Brien tells Winston that if the Party says a person can float off the ground, then it's true. This exemplifies the Party's belief in its own infallibility and its assertion that power lies in defining and controlling reality.

In all of these conflicts, the omnipresent shadow of Big Brother looms large, a symbol of the Party's watchful eyes and the suffocating grip it has on every aspect of life in Oceania. The various conflicts serve to elucidate the lengths to which totalitarian regimes can go to maintain power, control reality, and suppress dissent.

Climax and resolution

George Orwell wrote the climax and resolution to play a critical role in reinforcing the novel's bleak and unsettling themes.

Climax:

The climax of the novel occurs in the dreaded Room 101 within the Ministry of Love. Here, the Party confronts individuals with their worst fears, breaking their spirit and ensuring their absolute obedience. For Winston, his overwhelming terror is rats. O'Brien, who has been overseeing Winston's "reeducation," uses this fear against him.

Winston, strapped to a chair with a cage containing ravenous rats placed in front of his face, is pushed to the ultimate limit of his endurance. When the cage is opened, and the rats are about to be let loose on him, Winston, in his desperation to escape this nightmare, betrays Julia, screaming for them to "do it to Julia!" rather than him. This moment marks the completion of Winston's psychological torture and the ultimate destruction of his individual rebellion against the Party.

Reference:

"Do it to Julia! Do it to Julia! Not me! Julia! I don't care what you do to her. Tear her face off, strip her to the bones. Not me! Julia! Not me!"

Resolution:

Following his release from the Ministry of Love, Winston is a changed man. He spends his days at the Chestnut Tree Café, drinking Victory Gin and playing chess. The passionate rebel who sought to undermine the Party has been replaced with a subdued, broken individual who now loves Big Brother. Winston's internal resistance has been entirely crushed, signifying the Party's complete victory.

One of the most poignant scenes in the resolution is when Winston and Julia meet by chance in a park. Both acknowledge, with a mixture of guilt and resignation, that they betrayed each other under torture. This encounter underscores the depth of the Party's victory: it has not just broken their spirits but also destroyed the love they had for each other.

The novel concludes with a grim affirmation of the Party's total dominance over the individual mind and spirit:

"He loved Big Brother."

This chilling resolution serves as a powerful commentary on the lengths to which a totalitarian regime will go to maintain control and suppress individual thought and emotion. It underscores Orwell's warning about the dangers of unchecked power and the vulnerability of the human spirit when subjected to extreme manipulation and torture.

Moral lessons

"1984" by George Orwell is a complex and multi-faceted work, and its morals are manifold. However, some key messages can be discerned from the novel:

1. **The Dangers of Totalitarianism**: The most direct moral warning from the novel is against the dangers of unchecked governmental power and the erosion of individual rights. Orwell presents a dystopian world where the state has total control over every aspect of people's lives, including their thoughts, and uses it to caution against the rise of similar regimes in the real world.

2. **The Power and Malleability of Truth**: The novel frequently emphasizes the adage that "He who controls the past controls the future. He who controls the present controls the past." The constant rewriting of history by the Party illustrates how those in power can manipulate the truth to fit their narrative, leading to a society where objective reality is uncertain.

3. **The Importance of Individual Thought and Integrity**: Despite the overwhelming oppression in the novel, Winston's initial rebellion symbolizes the inherent human desire for freedom, truth, and individuality. The story serves as a reminder of the importance of preserving our individual rights to think and express freely.

4. **The Fragility of Human Loyalty under Extreme Pressure**: One of the novel's tragic aspects is the breaking of human bonds and loyalties under torture and fear. Winston and Julia's ultimate betrayals of one another in Room 101 underscore the lengths to which totalitarian regimes can go to destroy personal loyalties and relationships.

5. **Language as a Tool of Control**: Orwell introduces the concept of Newspeak, a language designed by the Party to eliminate unorthodox thoughts. This emphasizes the profound connection between language, thought, and freedom. When we allow language to be manipulated, we also allow our thoughts and freedoms to be constrained.

6. **The Human Need for Privacy**: The omnipresence of the Party, epitomized by the slogan "BIG BROTHER IS WATCHING YOU," showcases the invasive nature of surveillance. The novel warns about the psychological and societal effects of living under constant observation and the loss of private space, both physical and mental.

7. **The Potential Misuse of Technology**: While "1984" isn't strictly about technology, the use of telescreens, microphones, and other monitoring tools demonstrates how technology can be employed as an instrument of control and repression when wielded by a malicious entity.

In essence, "1984" serves as a profound cautionary tale about the vulnerabilities of society and the human spirit when confronted with unchecked power, manipulation, and oppression. It's a call to always be vigilant and to value and protect our individual freedoms and truths.

Famous lines

Here are some famous lines from "1984" by George Orwell, along with references to where they can be found within the novel:

1. **"War is peace. Freedom is slavery. Ignorance is strength."**

    ○ Part 1, Chapter 1: This paradoxical slogan of the Party is displayed on the white pyramid of the Ministry of Truth.

2. **"BIG BROTHER IS WATCHING YOU."**

    ○ Part 1, Chapter 1: This phrase is noted by Winston as being on a large poster that catches his eye as he enters his apartment building.

3. **"Who controls the past controls the future: who controls the present controls the past."**

    ○ Part 1, Chapter 3: Winston reflects on this Party mantra as he thinks about the mutability of the past.

4. **"Doublethink means the power of holding two contradictory beliefs in one's mind simultaneously, and accepting both of them."**

    ○ Part 2, Chapter 9: This definition is found in "The Theory and Practice of Oligarchical Collectivism," the book within the novel.

5. **"If you want a picture of the future, imagine a boot stamping on a human face—forever."**

   ○ Part 3, Chapter 3: O'Brien utters this to Winston during one of their confrontations in the Ministry of Love.

6. **"Don't you see that the whole aim of Newspeak is to narrow the range of thought? In the end, we shall make thoughtcrime literally impossible, because there will be no words in which to express it."**

   ○ Part 1, Chapter 5: Syme, who works on the Eleventh Edition of the Newspeak dictionary, explains this to Winston during their lunch break.

7. **"We shall meet in the place where there is no darkness."**

   ○ Part 1, Chapter 8: O'Brien says this cryptic line to Winston in a dream, and it later resurfaces during their actual interactions.

8. **"In the face of pain, there are no heroes."**

   ○ Part 3, Chapter 2: O'Brien speaks this line as he tortures Winston, highlighting the breaking point of every individual.

9. **"He loved Big Brother."**

   ○ Part 3, Chapter 6: The last line of the novel, signifying Winston's indoctrination and the complete victory of the Party over his individual will.

These references are based on the conventional chapter breakdowns in most editions of "1984." The context around each quote within the narrative enhances its significance and underscores Orwell's criticisms of totalitarian regimes and their mechanisms of control.

www.ingramcontent.com/pod-product-compliance
Lightning Source LLC
Chambersburg PA
CBHW071156120626
46546CB00006B/2299